Mock Meat

By: Julian Holden

Please Note

ISBN-13: 978-1542930017
ISBN-10: 1542930014

Contents

iv

Important Recommendations!   146

1. **Vegalcious Meatloaf bites**

Ingredients

- ❖ 15 ¾ oz of tempeh coarsely grated after boiling
- ❖ 4 small onions coarsely chopped
- ❖ 3 teaspoons chopped garlic
- ❖ 1 cup rolled oatmeal
- ❖ 1 cup of wheat gluten
- ❖ 1 ½ teaspoon of fennel seed, grounded
- ❖ 1 ½ teaspoon of sage, grounded
- ❖ 1 ½ teaspoon of thyme
- ❖ 1 ½ teaspoon of oregano, grounded
- ❖ 1 ½ teaspoon of parsley, finely chopped
- ❖ 1 ½ teaspoon of marjoram, grounded
- ❖ 9 teaspoons soy sauce
- ❖ 6 teaspoons HP brown sauce
- ❖ 6 teaspoons barbecue sauce
- ❖ 6 teaspoons olive oil
- ❖ 177 ml water

Glaze

- ❖ 158 ml ketchup
- ❖ 1 cup of brown sugar
- ❖ 1 ½ teaspoon of mustard

Directions

1. Start by greasing a 23x33-cm baking pan and preheat the oven to 177 degrees Celsius.

2. Add the oatmeal, garlic, onion, tempeh, sage, thyme, oregano, parsley, marjoram, and wheat gluten in a large-sized bowl and mix properly.

3. Slowly add the soy sauce, brown sauce, barbecue sauce, olive oil, and water and mash what you have recently added using your fingers. Mix well.

4. Prepare the greased pan. Split the mixed dough into pieces and form it into loaves, then place it in the greased pan.

5. Mix the ketchup, sugar, and mustard together. Use the mixture as a topping in every loaf created.

6. Place the pan in the over and set to an hour. Remove from the oven when the topping gets dark.

2.   <u>Vegan Meatballs</u>

Ingredients

- ❖ 6 teaspoons of olive oil
- ❖ 2 small sliced onions
- ❖ 1 large minced garlic clove
- ❖ 1 cup of heated walnuts
- ❖ 2 cups of cooked rice
- ❖ ¾ tablespoon of garden-fresh parsley
- ❖ 1 ½ teaspoon of dried basil
- ❖ ¾ teaspoon of grounded oregano
- ❖ ½ teaspoon of grounded sage
- ❖ ½ teaspoon of chili powder
- ❖ 8 pinches of salt
- ❖ 6 teaspoons of chickpea flour

Directions

1. Start by preheating the oven to 380 degrees Fahrenheit and let the parchment paper ready.

2. Heat the oil in a large pan on a low heat. Sauté garlic and onion till golden brown do this for about 16 minutes. Mix the rest until soft on a food mixer. Pour garlic-onion combination and wait until combined.

3. Take out a scooper or a spoon and heap out a mixture. Roll the mixture to make balls and put it on the baking sheet. Bake the meatballs until crisp and brown. Serve right away or place it in a fridge for a maximum of four days.

3. Bean Cakes A la Coconut

4 servings

Ingredients

- ❖ 6 teaspoons of olive oil
- ❖ 2 small chopped onions
- ❖ 1 chopped and seeded red bell pepper
- ❖ ¾ cup of celery, chopped
- ❖ 3 small minced garlic
- ❖ ¾ teaspoons of sweet paprika
- ❖ ¼ teaspoons of grounded thyme
- ❖ 1 ¾ cup of cooked kidney beans
- ❖ 3/4 cup of brown or white rice
- ❖ 6 teaspoons of minced parsley
- ❖ 2/3 cup of drained raw cashews
- ❖ 1 cup of coconut milk (unsweetened)
- ❖ A pinch of salt
- ❖ A pinch of ground black pepper

Directions

1. Heat 3 teaspoons of olive oil in a skillet over a low heat. Add bell pepper, onion, celery, paprika, garlic, cayenne, and thyme. While cooking, stir it occasionally until smooth for about 15 minutes. Add pepper and salt for seasoning.

2. Mix the salt, pepper, parsley, beans, rice and the others in a mixer. Reserve the ¼ cup of onion for the sauce. Pound the rice and bean mixture but leave some texture and shape it

into 4 pieces of patties. Add ground nuts, bread crumbs or oats if the mixture is still soft.

3. Take another 3 teaspoons of olive oil and heat on low heat. Cook the bean cakes until crisp and brown. Lower the heat to keep warm, while preparing the sauce.

4. Grind the reserved ¼ cup of onion and cashews in a mixer. Add pepper, salt and 1 cup of coconut milk. Increase the amount of coconut milk if you want a thinner sauce. Cook and stir the sauce into the saucepan on low heat. Place the bean cakes to a dish, pour over the sauce, and serve.

4.   **Vegan Sausages**

Ingredients

Dry

- ❖ 1/2 cup of vital wheat gluten flour
- ❖ 9 teaspoons of nutritional yeast
- ❖ 6 teaspoons of white flour
- ❖ ¾ teaspoon of flax meal
- ❖ 1 teaspoon of caraway seeds
- ❖ ¾ teaspoon of dry mustard
- ❖ ¾ teaspoon of celery seeds
- ❖ ¾ teaspoon of ground coriander
- ❖ ¾ teaspoon of ground paprika
- ❖ ¾ teaspoon of kosher salt
- ❖ ½ teaspoon of black pepper

Wet

- ❖ ¾ lb of drained extra firm tofu
- ❖ ½ cup of beer
- ❖ 3 teaspoons of minced red onion
- ❖ 3 teaspoons of finely chopped parsley
- ❖ 1 ¾ teaspoon of soy sauce
- ❖ 2 ¼ teaspoon of olive oil

Directions

1. Beat all the non-wet ingredients in a bowl. Put the mixture on one side.
2. With a medium-sized mixing bowl, crush the firm tofu and then add the beer, onion, parsley, soy sauce, and olive oil. Slowly mix the reserved mixture in the mixing bowl and stir.

3. Continue stirring for about 5 minutes to form structure.

4. When the mixture is already well-mixed, form the sausage by rolling each mixture using a parchment paper sealed by twisting the ends. Steam the sausage around 20-25 minutes using a steamer of your choice. After steaming, these sausages can be refrigerated or grilled.

5. Grill the sausages on a low heat for 7-12 minutes. Grilling the sausages can heat the sausages, offer a grill aroma, and can provide a crispy texture. Indirect heating works too because the sausages are a bit delicate to turn. Use a spatula for it works better than the tongs.

6. Serve the sausages on buns and try adding some of your favorite flavorings. Try adding relish, mustard, onions, sauerkraut, horseradish, sriracha, or simply ketchup. Refrigerate the sausages up to three days.

5. Lentil and Sweet Potato Burgers

Ingredients

- ❖ ¾ cup of cooked red lentils
- ❖ ½ cup of cooked quinoa
- ❖ ¾ cup of roasted sweet potato flesh
- ❖ 9 teaspoons of hemp seeds
- ❖ 6 teaspoons of ground flaxseed
- ❖ 6 teaspoons of curry powder
- ❖ ¾ teaspoon of smoked paprika
- ❖ 1 teaspoon of Indian spice mix
- ❖ ½ teaspoon of salt
- ❖ 6 teaspoons of chopped cilantro

Directions

1. Preheat the oven to 370 degrees
2. Combine mashed potato, quinoa, and red lentils on a huge container.
3. Add the remaining ingredients and stir to mix and set aside for 6 minutes.
4. Place a parchment sheet on a cookie tray and sprinkle with non-stick spray.
5. Create 8 to 10 burger patties with slightly damp hands.
6. Put the burger patties on the cookie tray.
7. Bake it for 18 minutes.
8. Turn the burgers to the other side and wait until they look crispy.

9. Remove the burger patties from the oven and let it cool before consumption. If you want it to store, place it in a sealed container. It can last for 7 days.

6.   Seitan & Waffle Breakfast with Pomegranate Sauce

Ingredients

For the pomegranate syrup

- ❖   1 ¼ cup of pure maple syrup
- ❖   ½ cup of pomegranate molasses

For the waffles

- ❖   1 ¾ cups of non-dairy milk
- ❖   3 teaspoons of cornstarch
- ❖   3 teaspoons of apple-cider vinegar
- ❖   2 ¼ cups of all-purpose flour
- ❖   9 teaspoons of sugar
- ❖   3 teaspoons of baking powder
- ❖   ¼ teaspoon of salt
- ❖   ¼ cup of water
- ❖   6 teaspoons of canola oil
- ❖   ¾ teaspoon of vanilla extract

For the chicken

- ❖   1 ¼ lb of Chicken-style Seitan

Batter

- ❖   9 teaspoons of flour
- ❖   6 teaspoons of cornstarch
- ❖   1 ¼ cup of water

Breading

- ❖   2 cups of breadcrumbs
- ❖   1 ¾ teaspoons of dried thyme
- ❖   ¾ teaspoon of salt

- ❖ ¾ teaspoon of black pepper
- ❖ ½ litre of vegetable oil

Directions

Making the syrup

1. To make the syrup, simply mix the pomegranate molasses and maple syrup in a cup. Set aside.

Making the waffles

2. With the aid of a measuring cup, dissolve the cornstarch in a half amount of milk. When it is dissolved, pour the remaining amount of milk in the measuring cup and add vinegar and mix. Reserve the mixture for the next procedure.
3. Combine the baking flour, sugar, salt, and flour in a medium-sized bowl and mix well.
4. Slowly add the previous mixture together with oil, vanilla, and water. Mix thoroughly the batter until it is smooth.
5. Prepare the waffle iron. And pour in the batter when the waffle iron is ready. Do not forget to use cooking spray to avoid any problems when making the waffle.

Making the chicken

6. With the use of a sharp knife, cut the seitan into slices.
7. Prepare the batter by mixing cornstarch, flour, and water in a medium-sized bowl. Mix thoroughly until it is smooth. On the other

hand, start mixing the thyme, pepper, salt, and breadcrumbs in a large plate.

8. Now, add some pepper, salt, thyme, and bread crumbs. Mix them together.

9. With the sliced seitan earlier, dip it into the batter and transfer to the bowl of bread crumbs. Coat it completely. Fry the seitan slices once all of them are coated in bread crumbs.

10. Heat the skillet over a medium-high heat and pour a half-full of oil on the skillet. When the oil is hot enough, dip the pieces into the oil until it gets the color golden brown. Prepare paper towels on a plate and put the fried seitan to drain the vegetable oil. If there are more, then repeat the steps.

11. When done, serve the seitan slices over a waffle and garnish with abundant syrup.

7. <u>Seitan Steak & Sautéed Mushrooms</u>

Seitan

Gluten

- ❖ 2 ¼ cups of vital wheat gluten
- ❖ 4 teaspoons of nutritional yeast
- ❖ ¾ teaspoon of kosher salt
- ❖ ¾ teaspoon of mustard powder
- ❖ ¾ black pepper
- ❖ 2 ¼ cups of water
- ❖ ¾ teaspoon of vegan Worcestershire sauce

Broth

- ❖ 8 ½ cups of veggie broth
- ❖ ¾ cup of red wine
- ❖ 4 teaspoons of nutritional yeast
- ❖ 1 ¾ teaspoon of peppercorns
- ❖ 2 teaspoon of vegan Worcestershire sauce
- ❖ ¾ teaspoon of salt
- ❖ ¾ teaspoon of mustard powder
- ❖ ¾ teaspoon of onion powder
- ❖ ½ teaspoon of dried thyme

Directions

1. Combine the yeast, mustard, gluten, pepper, and salt in a bowl. Mix the Worcestershire sauce and the water and add it to the gluten. Massage it for around 6 minutes. Boil all broth ingredients and stir. Slice the pressed gluten to a half an inch using a knife. Put the sliced

glutens into the hot broth, cover and let it simmer for 1 hour and 15 minutes while mixing every 15 minutes.

2. Place a vegan butter on a pan and sauté the Seitan steaks when done cooking into the broth.

Braised Mushrooms

- ❖ ¾ lb of sliced cremini mushrooms
- ❖ 3 teaspoons of finely chopped garlic
- ❖ 3 tablespoons of olive oil
- ❖ 3 teaspoons of lemon juice
- ❖ ¾ teaspoon of kosher salt
- ❖ ¼ tablespoon of dill
- ❖ 1 teaspoon of black pepper

3. Throw all ingredients into the skillet and bake it in a 325-degree Fahrenheit oven for 1 hour and 30 mins, just as the time for the mushrooms to be cooked.

8.   Spicy Barbecue Lentil "Loaf"

50 minutes preparation time
1 hour and 50 minutes cooking time
2 hours and 40 minutes total

Ingredients

To make the lentils

- ❖ ¾ cup of green lentils
- ❖ ¾ teaspoon of sea salt

Lentil batter remaining ingredients

- ❖ ¾ cup of chopped onion
- ❖ 3 teaspoons of minced garlic
- ❖ ½ teaspoon of sea salt
- ❖ ½ cup of water
- ❖ ¾ cup of barbecue sauce
- ❖ ¾ cup of cornmeal, medium grind
- ❖ 9 teaspoons of ground flaxseed
- ❖ 1 teaspoon of chipotle chili
- ❖ ¾ cup of corn

Homemade Barbecue Sauce

- ❖ ¾ cup of tomato paste
- ❖ ¾ cup of water
- ❖ ¾ teaspoon of sea salt
- ❖ 4 teaspoons of garlic powder
- ❖ 4 teaspoons of chili powder
- ❖ 4 teaspoons of wet mustard
- ❖ 4 teaspoons of maple syrup
- ❖ 8 teaspoons of dark balsamic vinegar
- ❖ 8 teaspoons of regular unsulphured molasses

Directions

1. This recipe would take about 2 to 3 hours of preparation and cooking. You can cook the lentils a day before you make this recipe to save more time.

2. To make the barbecue sauce, mix the listed ingredients above well until thickened. Store in the refrigerator overnight.

3. With the ½ cup of water and (2) ¼ teaspoons of salt, add the rinsed lentils to the pot and boil. Do this for about half an hour. Let the water inside the pot evaporate. Remove the pot from the stove and set aside for 15 minutes.

4. Now, sauté the garlic and onions by adding ¾ cup of water and (2) 1/8 teaspoon of salt with the garlic and onions to a frying pan. Boil and simmer around 5-10 minutes or let the water evaporate.

5. Place half of the lentils in a blender and slowly mash it. Now, add the mixture, including the other half, in a large-sized bowl.

6. Prepare the oven by preheating it to 355 degrees Fahrenheit. Cover a metal loaf pan with a parchment paper making sure that it can be removed easily later. You can use cooking spray on the pan so that the paper does not stick.

7. Add ¾ cup of barbecue sauce together with the cooked onion and garlic to the lentil mixture. Mix in the chipotle chili and a pinch of salt. Mix thoroughly.

8. Slowly add the flaxseed and cornmeal to the mixture and stir. This makes the mixture sticky and thick. Put the corn into the mixture and stir.

9. With the mixture done, slowly pour it into the loaf pan and spread evenly. Set aside for 25 minutes. Layer the mixture with ¾ cup of barbecue sauce. Bake for an hour.

10. Let the loaf sit for about 20 to 25 minutes for it to become firm. Grab the sides of the parchment paper to remove the loaf from the pan. Transfer the loaf to a platter. Slice the loaf and lay some barbecue sauce just before it cools.

9. <u>Nut Rice "loaf" & Vegan Cheese Sauce</u>

Ingredients

- ❖ ¼ cup of brown rice
- ❖ 1 ¼ cup of water
- ❖ 3 teaspoons of olive oil
- ❖ 2 chopped small onions
- ❖ ¾ cup of grounded raw cashews
- ❖ 2 cups of dry breadcrumbs
- ❖ 1 ¼ cup of nut milk
- ❖ 6 teaspoons of fresh parsley
- ❖ 3 teaspoons of soy sauce
- ❖ 8 pinches of salt
- ❖ 3 teaspoons of olive oil

Directions

1. To start cooking the rice, pour the uncooked rice together with water and place it a sauce pan over low heat and let it simmer about 50 minutes.

2. Set aside the cooked rice, and start pouring 3 teaspoons of olive oil in a frying pan over a medium heat. Then, sauté onion for about 10 minutes making sure it is not overcooked. When it's done, place the onion in a large-sized bowl.

3. Using a mixing bowl, mix the cooled onion with the loaf ingredient. Add the cooked rice to the mixture and combine well. Add some breadcrumbs if the mixture is still wet.

4. If the loaf mixture blended well, set this aside and start heating the oven to 360 degrees Fahrenheit. Move the mixed cashew to an oiled loaf pan and start baking it for 50 minutes or until the color on top of the loaf has become brown.

Red pepper cheese sauce

- ❖ 6 chopped and seeded small orange bell peppers
- ❖ ¾ cup of chopped cashews
- ❖ 2 cups of water
- ❖ 3 tablespoons of olive oil
- ❖ 16-20 pinches of salt
- ❖ 3 teaspoons of nutritional yeast
- ❖ ½ teaspoon of garlic powder
- ❖ ½ teaspoon of black/white pepper

5. Mix all ingredients in a blender for up to 3 minutes.

6. After blending, transfer it to a saucepan and cook the mixture on a low heat for 30 mins until bubbly and thick. While cooking, stir to refrain the mixture from sticking to the pan.

7. Cook the spices and pepper and cook the cashews lightly so that it will be thick.

8. Once done, serve this sauce on the rice loaf or your special meals.

10.   <u>Bean & Broccoli Meatballs</u>

15 mins to prepare
30 mins to cook
A total of 45 mins

Ingredients

- ❖ ¾ lb of chopped and rapini with stems removed
- ❖ 2 chopped small onions
- ❖ 1 ½ teaspoon of minced garlic
- ❖ 2 cups of cooked cannellini beans
- ❖ 1 ¼ cups of plain bread crumbs
- ❖ ¾ teaspoon of Italian seasoning
- ❖ ½ teaspoon of salt
- ❖ ½ teaspoon of black pepper
- ❖ 3 teaspoons olive oil
- ❖ Mariner's sauce

Directions

1. Set the oven to 204 degrees Celsius.
2. While waiting for the oven to have the right temperature, steam the rapini for 2 ½ minutes just until the rapini is lightly tender. Set aside and let it cool.
3. Together with the garlic, onion, breadcrumbs, Italian seasoning, and beans, mix it with the steamed rapini.
4. Slightly mash the beans and beat until mixed wholly. Scrape and form into balls (around 20-24 balls)

5. Coat the baking pan with 1 ½ teaspoons of olive oil and put the meatballs on it. Apply the remaining oil on the meatball

6. Bake them for 25 minutes while making sure that all sides are evenly baked. When done, serve it with mariner's sauce.

11. **Black Bean Quinoa Burgers**

30 minutes to prepare
40 minutes to cook
A total of 1 hour and 15 minutes
10 to 15 patties depending on the size

Ingredients

- ❖ 6 teaspoons of flaxseed with 6 tablespoons of water
- ❖ 3 teaspoons of olive oil
- ❖ ¾ cup of fresh quinoa
- ❖ 1 chopped small onion
- ❖ 1 chopped bell pepper
- ❖ 1 chopped and seeded jalapeño pepper
- ❖ 3 minced garlic cloves
- ❖ 1 ¼ cup of chopped spinach
- ❖ 2 cups of cooked black beans
- ❖ ¾ teaspoon of salt
- ❖ ¾ teaspoon of paprika
- ❖ ¾ teaspoon of cumin
- ❖ ¾ teaspoon of pepper
- ❖ ¼ teaspoon of ground cayenne
- ❖ 1 cup of oat flour

Directions

1. While greasing the baking sheet, heat the oven to 360 degrees Fahrenheit. Also, place the water-flax meal mixture inside the refrigerator.

2. Heat a teaspoon of olive oil in a pan. Set the heat to low heat. Before adding the quinoa, rinse it first. Once the oil is heated, cook the

quinoa until crisp. Add 2 cups of water and increase the heat. Once it starts boiling; lessen the heat, cover the pan and let it boil for 14-16 minutes.

3. On another pan heat a tablespoon of olive oil. Add the sliced onion and cook for 2 minutes. Add jalapeño, garlic, and bell pepper and wait for the onion to look shine. Put some spinach and mix right away. Turn it off after somewhat wilt.

4. On a large container, mix mashed black beans, salt, quinoa, vegetables, paprika, pepper, cumin, flax seeds, and cayenne. Lastly, add the oat flour and stir to combine.

5. Fill the baking sheet with patties, bake both sides of the patties for 25 minutes or until patties are crisp and golden brown.

6. Add a barbecue sauce, toppings, guacamole on a wheat burger bun and serve.

12. **<u>Vegan "Turkey" Deli Slices</u>**

Ingredients

- ❖ 1 cup of white cannellini beans
- ❖ 3 teaspoons olive oil
- ❖ 1 ½ cup of water
- ❖ 6 teaspoons of soy sauce
- ❖ 1 tablespoon of vegan Worcester sauce
- ❖ 4 tablespoons of nutritional yeast
- ❖ ½ teaspoon of onion powder
- ❖ ½ teaspoon of smoked sea salt
- ❖ ½ teaspoon of grounded sage
- ❖ ½ teaspoon of grounded thyme
- ❖ 1 ¾ cups of wheat gluten

Directions

1. Mix the yeast, salt, species, and onion powder in a bowl. Crush the mixture until the mixture becomes powder-like. Set Aside.

2. Put in the beans and slowly mash just before the mixture is creamy.

3. Using a measuring cup, mix the olive oil, soy sauce, water, and the Worcester sauce. Gently whisk in the seasonings and the yeast. Gradually add the liquid on top of the beans, whisk until fully mix.

4. Scatter some wheat gluten, mix and press until you have made a loaf.

5. Steam the loaf for 50 minutes while it is wrapped in a foil. Check the level of water as to not dry the loaf.

6. Heat the oven to 200 degrees Celsius when 10 minutes is left when steaming. Bake the loaf in the oven for 35 minutes. Remove the loaf and slice once it is cooled.

13.   <u>Vegan Chickpea Burgers</u>

Serves 4-6 patties

Ingredients

- ❖ 6 teaspoons of sesame seeds
- ❖ 2 small onions
- ❖ 1 medium size carrot
- ❖ 2 stalks of celery
- ❖ 1 small garlic clove
- ❖ 1 cup cooked beans
- ❖ ¾ cup of cooked cracked wheat
- ❖ 3 teaspoons of soy sauce
- ❖ 1 teaspoon of curry powder
- ❖ 1.5 teaspoon of ground cumin
- ❖ 1 teaspoon of cardamom or coriander
- ❖ ½ teaspoon of smoked paprika
- ❖ ¼ teaspoon of pepper
- ❖ ¾ teaspoon of salt
- ❖ ½ cup of potato or other flour

Instructions

1. Using a fry pan, heat sesame seeds until brown and they start to pop. Set aside.
2. Cut the chickpeas leaving some portions uncut. Add to the sesame seeds then set aside.
3. Blend the carrot, celery, and onion.
4. Using a blender, pulse the vegetables but do not overdo.
5. After pulsing, add the vegetables to a medium-sized bowl together with the chickpeas and sesame seeds.

6. Add and mix the remaining ingredients.
7. Add three teaspoons of flour at a time if the patties are not firm enough.
8. Slowly shape the mixture into patties and cook in a frying pan.
9. After cooking, pair it up with a burger bun together with flavorings according to your choice.

14. <u>Apple Seitan</u>

Ingredients

- ❖ 1.5 cup of vegetable broth
- ❖ 3 small sweet onions
- ❖ 3 minced garlic cloves
- ❖ 4 small chopped apples
- ❖ Herbed seitan recipe
- ❖ ¼ teaspoon of dried rosemary
- ❖ ¾ teaspoon of dried thyme leaves
- ❖ ¾ teaspoon of dried marjoram
- ❖ ¼ teaspoon dried sage
- ❖ 3 pinches of pepper and salt
- ❖ ¾ cup of fresh basil chiffonade

Directions

1. In a pan, sauté garlic and onion with a small amount of vegetable broth over low-medium heat just before the onion softens.
2. Put on the herbs and chopped apples to the pan just until the apples break down.
3. Slowly add the basil and seitan to the pan and stir.
4. Cook for about 4-6 minutes making sure that the seitan is heated.

15. Mushroom "Bacon"

Ingredients

- ❖ 8 ounces of shiitake mushrooms
- ❖ 1.5 teaspoon of soy sauce
- ❖ 1/8 cup of olive oil

Directions

1. Pre-heat the oven to 360 degrees Fahrenheit.
2. Stem and slice the mushrooms into one-fourth inch slices. Add the mushrooms together with the olive oil and soy sauce.
3. Using a parchment baking paper, evenly place the mushrooms in a layer and bake for about 15-25 minutes.

16. __Thanks giving Meatless Loaf__

Preparation Time: 25 minutes
Cooking Time: 1 hour and 10 minutes
Total time: 1 hour and 35 minutes
Serving: 8 persons

Ingredients

- ❖ 2 small sweet potatoes
- ❖ 2 small onions
- ❖ 3 ribs of celery
- ❖ 2 small carrots
- ❖ 1 garlic cloves, chopped
- ❖ 1.75 cups of drained cannellini beans
- ❖ 15 oz of extra-firm tofu
- ❖ 6 teaspoons of coconut aminos or gluten free soy sauce
- ❖ 6 teaspoons of tomato paste
- ❖ 3 teaspoons of mustard
- ❖ ¼ cup chopped parsley
- ❖ 1.5 teaspoon of rubbed sage
- ❖ 3 teaspoons of thyme leaf
- ❖ 1.5 teaspoon of crushed dried rosemary
- ❖ 1 teaspoon of salt
- ❖ ¼ teaspoon of black pepper
- ❖ 1 ½ teaspoon smoked paprika
- ❖ 6 teaspoons of nutritional yeast
- ❖ 1 cup of flakes or oatmeal

Directions

1. Start by thoroughly washing the potato and piercing it using a fork. Then, wrap the potato using a paper towel and put it in the microwave

for 5-6 minutes. Let it cool for a few minutes then peel the potato. Set aside.

2. Finely chop the carrot, celery, and onion.

3. Using a large frying pan, add the chopped vegetables together with the garlic and cook for about 8-15 minutes until tender. On the other hand, drain the beans and smash them tenderly using a spoon.

4. With the use of a food processor, add the potato together with the soy sauce, seasonings, tofu, and yeast. Do this until you have a fair and smooth mixture. Mix in the walnuts and pulse. Place the mixture into a large-sized mixing bowl and add the cook vegetables. Mix well.

5. Prepare the oven by preheating it to 370 degrees Fahrenheit. Place a parchment paper on the baking sheet. Using your hands, shape a loaf out of the tofu mixture you have, about 2 ¾ inches in height and place it on the baking surface. Bake for about 30 minutes. Roughly cover the loaf using aluminum foil and cook for 15 minutes more. When it's done, let it cool for about 15 minutes before slicing.

17. Coconut Fried Seitan with Mushrooms

Ingredients

- ❖ 500 ml of vegetable oil
- ❖ ¾ tin of seitan, chopped into chunks
- ❖ 1 ¼ cup of button mushrooms
- ❖ 4 tablespoons of tamari
- ❖ ½ teaspoon of red pepper flakes
- ❖ ½ stalk of lemongrass with chopped ends
- ❖ ½ tablespoon of grated ginger

For the dry dredge

- ❖ ¼ cup of corn flour with pepper, salt, garlic powder, and cayenne pepper

For the batter

- ❖ 1 cup of coconut milk
- ❖ ¾ cup of cornflour
- ❖ ½ tablespoon of baking soda

For the crumb layer

- ❖ ¾ cup of bread crumbs
- ❖ ¾ cup of desiccated coconut

Directions

1. In a medium-sized bowl, put the mushrooms and seitan together with the red pepper flakes, lemon grass, tamari, and use a cling film to cover it. Marinate for about 50-60 minutes. Mix the ingredients for the dry dredge in a flat

dish and start whisking the batter ingredients in a medium-sized mixing bowl.

2. Sprinkle the desiccated coconut and panko in a dish. Preheat a pan over a medium heat and add the oil. Start with a piece of mushroom or seitan and plunge it into the dredge coating thoroughly to make the batter stick. Slowly dip it to the batter mixture and place it in the crumb mixture. Now, place it in the pan. Fry it for about 5 minutes. Dry off some excess oil using a kitchen paper towel then serve.

18.   Teriyaki Seitan and Broccolini

Serving: 2 persons

Ingredients

- ❖ 10 oz of sliced seitan
- ❖ 1 ½ cup of sushi rice, uncooked
- ❖ 7 to 9 broccolini stalks
- ❖ 3 Clementines
- ❖ 3 teaspoons vegetable oil
- ❖ A bottle of Teriyaki Sauce added with Clementine zest
- ❖ ¼ cup of Tamari (low sodium)
- ❖ ½ cup of brown sugar
- ❖ ½ cup of clementine juice
- ❖ ½ cup of rice vinegar
- ❖ 1/3 cup of water
- ❖ Skin from a small clementine

Directions

1. Soak the sushi rice in a cool water and remove excess water. Cook the sushi rice in a rice cooker. After cooking, steam it for about 6-12 minutes off the heat.

2. Using a small-sized pan, mix all the sauce ingredients and let it simmer for about 25 minutes until it is thick. Once done, set aside.

3. Cut the seitan about 1" thick and prepare the broccolini.

4. Over a medium heat, heat a large-sized pan and add the seitan and cook for 3-6 minutes. Set

aside. Place the broccolini in the pan over a high heat. Cook for about 4-5 minutes.

5. In the pan, add the seitan and glaze some teriyaki sauce to coat it. Serve together with the sushi rice.

19. <u>Vegan Meatloaf & Mashed Potatoes</u>

Serving: 6 persons

Ingredients

Vegan Meat loaf

- ❖ 1.5 tablespoons of olive oil
- ❖ 3 small chopped onions
- ❖ ¾ cup chopped celery
- ❖ small chopped carrots
- ❖ 1.5 of vegetarian bouillon cubes
- ❖ 2 lbs of fresh mushrooms
- ❖ ¾ cup bell pepper (chopped)
- ❖ ½ block of tempeh
- ❖ 1.5 cup of sun-dried tomatoes (chopped)
- ❖ ¾ cup of chopped walnuts
- ❖ ½ cup ketchup
- ❖ 1 ¼ teaspoon mustard
- ❖ ¾ cup bread crumbs
- ❖ ¼ teaspoon garlic powder
- ❖ ½ teaspoon red pepper (crushed)
- ❖ ¼ teaspoon of dried thyme
- ❖ ¼ tablespoon paprika
- ❖ ½ cup of half and half
- ❖ A recipe for ketchup glaze

Directions

1. Start by preheating your oven to 360 degrees Fahrenheit. In a medium-sized pan, melt the butter over medium heat. Add in the celery,

carrot, and onion to the pan and cook for about 8 minutes then add the bouillon cubes and mix.

2. Place the mixture on a large-sized mixing bowl. Add the remaining ingredients in the mixture and mix it thoroughly. Set aside the mixture in the refrigerator for about 15 minutes.

3. Place the mixture in a Silpat-lined baking sheet. Form a loaf out of the mixture about 12" long, 8" wide, and 3" tall. Bake for about 30 minutes. Brush the loaf with ketchup glaze and bake it for another 15 minutes and repeat this process again.

Ketchup Glaze

- ❖ ¾ cup ketchup
- ❖ 3 teaspoons of soy sauce
- ❖ 2 teaspoons Tabasco
- ❖ 1.5 teaspoon black pepper
- ❖ 3 teaspoons sorghum

4. In a medium-sized mixing bowl, mix the ketchup glaze ingredients well and set aside.

Parsley and Tomato Salad

- ❖ 1 cup tomato (chopped)
- ❖ ¾ cup chopped parsley
- ❖ 1/3 cup diced shallot
- ❖ 2 pinches of salt
- ❖ 2 dashes of black pepper
- ❖ ¼ teaspoon sugar
- ❖ ¼ tablespoon champagne vinegar

5. Using a small-sized mixing bowl, add the ingredients and mix it all together. Set aside.

Garlic Mashed Potatoes

- ❖ 4 ½ cups of diced and peeled potatoes
- ❖ 3 cups chopped cauliflower
- ❖ 4 teaspoons olive oil
- ❖ ¾ cup of half and half
- ❖ 7 chopped garlic cloves
- ❖ ¼ tablespoon salt
- ❖ 1/8 teaspoon of pepper
- ❖ 1/3 cup sour cream

1. Place the ingredients in a small-sized microwave-safe bowl. Microwave it over high temperature for about 15 minutes. Mash the mixture with the use of a potato masher and then add the sour cream.

20. <u>Smoky Seitan</u>

Serves 4
Preparation Time: 20 minutes
Cooking Time: 2 hours and 10 minutes
Overall Time: 2 hours and 30 minutes

Ingredients

- ❖ 1 cup of wheat gluten
- ❖ 9 teaspoons of nutritional yeast
- ❖ 6 teaspoons of garlic powder
- ❖ 6 teaspoons of onion powder
- ❖ 1 ½ cup of water
- ❖ ½ cup of soy sauce
- ❖ 3 teaspoons of barbecue sauce
- ❖ 1 ½ tablespoon of brown sugar
- ❖ ½ tablespoon of chili powder
- ❖ 1/8 tablespoon of cayenne pepper
- ❖ 4 dashes of black pepper
- ❖ 2 ½ tablespoons of paprika
- ❖ 150 ml of barbecue sauce

Directions

1. In a large-sized bowl, mix the yeast, gluten, a tablespoon of onion and garlic powder.
2. Mix a tablespoon of barbecue and soy sauce added with water in another bowl.
3. Combine the two mixtures in one bowl.
4. Press for about 5-6 minutes. Let it rest for 8 minutes.
5. With the dough, stretch it for about 9-10" long and cut into 4 equal pieces.

6. Add cold water in a large-sized pot. Place the seitan into the water. Partly cover the pot and start boiling. When it starts boiling, let it simmer.

7. Cook for about 1 hour and 10 minutes. Let it cool when done.

8. Meanwhile, start mixing the spices.

9. Scrub the spice mixture to the cooled seitan pieces.

10. Prepare your grill and heat up coals and some wood.

11. Place the seitan pieces and smoke them for about 40-45 minutes.

12. Garnish the seitan pieces with the barbecue sauce and grill for about 6 more minutes.

13. Serve when done.

21. <u>Vegetarian Lentil Burger Recipe</u>

Ingredients

- ❖ 2 ½ cups of black lentils (cooked)
- ❖ 7 tablespoons Flax Seeds
- ❖ ¼ tablespoon sea salt
- ❖ 1 medium size chopped onion
- ❖ ¾ cup bread crumbs
- ❖ 3 teaspoons of olive oil

Directions

1. Using a food processor, mix the Flax Seeds, Lentils and salt. Transfer the mixture to a large-sized mixing bowl and add the onion. Add the breadcrumbs and mix well. Form 15 patties about 2" thick.

2. Prepare the pan by heating oil over medium heat. Place in 5 patties in the pan. Cover and cook for about 10-15 minutes. Remove the patties when it is already golden brown. Then cut in half and stuff in your chosen fillings.

22. **Baked Seiten Mix**

Dry ingredients

- ❖ 1 ½ cup of wheat gluten
- ❖ ¼ cup of chickpea flour
- ❖ 1 ½ tablespoon of nutritional yeast

Wet ingredients

- ❖ 3 tablespoons Worcestershire sauce, coconut aminos or soy-free tamari
- ❖ 1 ½ tablespoons of olive oil
- ❖ 1 ½ cup of water

Directions

1. Mix the dry ingredients in a large-sized mixing bowl. Slowly mix the wet ingredients. Knead to combine. Let it sit for at least 10 minutes.

Parsley Root (orcelery root , o parsnip) Stuffing

- ❖ 2 ½ cups of parsnip, celery root or parsley root (diced)
- ❖   ¼ cup of almond/hazelnut meal
- ❖ 6 teaspoons dijon mustard
- ❖ 3 teaspoons of dried thyme

2. Prepare your oven by preheating it to 340-400 degrees Fahrenheit.

3. Set aside the prepared seitan mixture and side dish.

4. Grease your baking sheet with vegetable oil and stretch the dough out making a large rectangle shape. Place the stretched dough on

the baking sheet and gradually press it until it becomes bigger.

5. Using a brush, top the dough with oil and place it in the oven. Bake for about 10 minutes.

6. In a small-sized pot, boil a small amount of water and add in the parsley root. Let it boil for about 8 minutes. Remove excess water.

7. Mix the hazelnut meal, thyme, mustard, and parsley root in a medium-sized bowl.

8. Put the seitan on a plate and place the prepared mixture in the center of the rectangle. Start rolling the shorter end towards the other end. Use a cotton string to tie the dough and stuff back fallen mixtures. Set aside.

9. Place the seitan back on the tray and brush some oil. Bake for around 30 minutes.

Miso Gravy

Serving: 4 persons

- ❖ 2 small onions
- ❖ 3 ½ tablespoons of gluten free flour
- ❖ 3 cups of water
- ❖ 5 teaspoons of miso
- ❖ 3 teaspoons of fresh thyme
- ❖ 1 teaspoon of fresh sage
- ❖ 1 teaspoon of fresh rosemary
- ❖ 2 pinches of cracked pepper
- ❖ ¼ teaspoon balsamic vinegar

10. Heat the olive oil in a skillet and add in the onion. Choose high heat and gradually stir the onions until tender. Slowly stir in the flour

followed by water. Make sure there are no lumps. Mix the miso, pepper, vinegar, and herbs and boil. Simmer for about 10 minutes.

23. Cajun Meatloaf with Sweet Glaze

Serves about 5-12 small-sized meatloaves.

Ingredients

- ❖ 16 ounces of grated tempeh
- ❖ 2 medium grated sweet onions
- ❖ 3 grated garlic cloves
- ❖ ½ cup of wheat gluten
- ❖ 3 teaspoons of paprika
- ❖ 1 tablespoon of sage
- ❖ 1 tablespoon of thyme
- ❖ ½ tablespoon of coriander
- ❖ 6 pinches of seasoned salt
- ❖ 3 dashes of cayenne pepper
- ❖ 3 teaspoons of soy sauce
- ❖ 6 teaspoons of HP sauce
- ❖ 1.5 tablespoon of olive oil

Glaze

- ❖ ¾ cup of ketchup
- ❖ 1/3 cup of brown sugar
- ❖ ¼ tablespoon of mustard
- ❖ 3 tablespoons of bourbon

Directions

1. Start by preheating the oven to 360 degrees Fahrenheit. Grease the baking pan.
2. In a large-sized mixing bowl, mix the onion, grated tempeh, flour, spices, and garlic.

3. Slowly add the oil and sauces. Mash for 5 minutes to mix well.

4. Split the dough into 12 pieces and form small-sized loaves. Put it into the greased pan and spray some oil. Bake for about 20 minutes.

5. Using a small-sized pan, boil the glaze ingredients. Let it thicken. Garnish it on top of the baking loaves. Bake for another 20 minutes more. Repeat the process again.

24. <u>Chickpea "Tuna" Salad</u>

Ingredients

- ❖ 420 grams can of chickpeas
- ❖ 2 celery stalks with leaves (chopped)
- ❖ 5 teaspoons of unsweetened pickle relish
- ❖ 5 dashes of dill, onion powder, parsley, old bay seasoning, and celery salt
- ❖ 3 dashes of black pepper
- ❖ 2 ½ tablespoons of vegan mayonnaise

Directions

1. Start by mashing the chickpeas thoroughly. Add in the remaining ingredients and mix them well. Place it in the fridge for a few minutes and serve.
2. Combine the chickpea tuna salad with veggies or lettuce.

25. <u>Classic Seitan</u>

Ingredients

ForSeitan

- ❖   2 ½ cup of vital wheat gluten
- ❖   3 tablespoons of flour
- ❖   1/3 cup of nutritional yeast
- ❖   ½ cup of vegetable broth
- ❖   ¾ cup of soy sauce
- ❖   2 teaspoons of ketchup
- ❖   3 teaspoons of olive oil
- ❖   1 ½ tablespoons of chickpea flour

For the broth

- ❖   10 cups of water
- ❖   2 cups of vegetable broth
- ❖   1/3 cup of soy sauce
- ❖   1 teaspoon of garlic powder
- ❖   1 teaspoon of onion powder

Directions

1. Mix the first three ingredients in a large-sized bowl. Set aside.

2. Mix in the vegetable broth, soy sauce, ketchup, and olive oil using a different bowl.

3. Add the wet ingredients to the dry ingredients and mix well.

4. Mash the chickpea flour and let it rest for 6 minutes.

5. Mix the broth ingredients using a large-sized pot.

6. On the other hand, start rolling the dough into 12" long and cut into 8 pieces.

7. Put the chopped pieces into the prepared cold broth. Partly cover and heat to medium. When it boils, lower the heat and let it simmer for about 2 hours.

8. Let it cool for another hour and a half.

26. "Cheeseburger" Lentil Loaf

Serving: 4 persons

Ingredients

- ❖ 1.5 cup of lentils (cooked)
- ❖ 2 cups of cooked rice
- ❖ 1/3 cup of breadcrumbs
- ❖ 1 medium size diced onion
- ❖ Half packet of meatloaf seasoning
- ❖ ¾ bag of nut cheese
- ❖ ½ cup of veganaise
- ❖ 1/8 cup of mustard
- ❖ ¼ cup of ketchup

Directions

1. Preheat the oven to 380 degrees Fahrenheit.
2. Mix the cooked rice and lentils in a large-sized mixing bowl.
3. Add the seasoning, breadcrumbs, Daiya cheese, mustard, onion, and veganaise.
4. Blend the mixture using a food processor. Make sure that the lentils are mashed properly.
5. Grease a loaf pan and plan the mixture shaping it into a loaf. Bake for 40-50 minutes.

27. <u>Seitan #2</u>

Ingredients

- ❖ 2 cups of wheat gluten
- ❖ 1/8 cup of nutritional yeast
- ❖ 6 pinches of salt
- ❖ ½ tablespoon of paprika
- ❖ ½ tablespoon of pepper
- ❖ 2 medium sized garlic cloves
- ❖ 3 medium sized basil leaves (chopped)
- ❖ 1 cup of cold water
- ❖ 1 tablespoon of tomato paste
- ❖ ½ tablespoon of olive oil
- ❖ ½ tablespoon of vegetable broth

Directions

1. Preheat the oven to 340 degrees Fahrenheit.
2. Mix all the dry ingredients in a large-sized mixing bowl. Mix thoroughly.
3. Then mix all the wet ingredients in a different bowl.
4. Add the wet ingredients to the dry ones and mix using your hands. Knead the mixture until mixed thoroughly.
5. Roll into a sausage shape and wrap it with 3 layers of aluminum foil with ends twisted.
6. Bake for 2 hours.

28. <u>Vegetarian Meatloaf</u>

Preparation Time: 30 minutes
Cooking Time: 1 hour and 10 minutes
Total Time: 1 hour and 50 minutes
Serving: 8 persons

Ingredients

- ❖ 10.5 ounces of bottle barbecue sauce
- ❖ 10.5 ounces of vegetarian burger crumbles
- ❖ 1 small chopped bell pepper
- ❖ ½ cup minced onion
- ❖ 1 medium sized minced garlic clove
- ❖ ¾ cup of bread crumbs
- ❖ 2 tablespoon of nut cheese
- ❖ 1 tablespoon of flax seed
- ❖ ½ teaspoon of dried thyme
- ❖ ½ teaspoon of dried basil
- ❖ ½ teaspoon of parsley flakes
- ❖ 4 pinches of pepper and salt

Directions

1. Grease a loaf pan and preheat the oven to 340 degrees Fahrenheit.

2. Mix a half ounce of barbecue sauce together with the burger crumbles, onion, garlic, bell pepper, nut cheese, flaxseed, and breadcrumbs. Season it with spices. Transfer the mixture to the greased loaf pan.

3. Bake the loaf for about 50 minutes. Garnish the remaining half of the barbecue sauce over the loaf and bake for another 20 minutes.

29. <u>Vegan Hot Dogs / Lil' Smokeys</u>

Preparation Time: 1 hour and 10 minutes
Cooking Time: 50 minutes
Servings: 25-40

Ingredients

- ❖ ¼ cup of rinsed and drained white beans
- ❖ ½ cup minced onion
- ❖ 1 medium sized minced garlic clove
- ❖ 1/8 tablespoon of coriander
- ❖ ½ teaspoon of dried marjoram
- ❖ ½ teaspoon of ground mace
- ❖ ¼ tablespoon of ground mustard seed
- ❖ ¼ tablespoon of paprika
- ❖ 5 dashes of pepper and salt
- ❖ 1 teaspoon or maple syrup or sugar
- ❖ ¾ cup of vegetable broth
- ❖ 3 teaspoons of olive oil
- ❖ 6 teaspoons of soy sauce
- ❖ ½ teaspoon of liquid smoke
- ❖ 1/3 cup of nutritional yeast
- ❖ 1 cup of wheat gluten

Directions

1. Using a food processor, mash beans until mush. Start mixing the garlic, onion, and spices. Prepare a steamer basket.
2. Add the oil, liquid smoke, soy sauce, broth, and yeast. Mix it properly. After, add the gluten.
3. Now, mix all the ingredients and form the dough into narrow strips.

4. Tear off aluminum foil sheets. Roll the strips with a foil and twist the ends to seal. Place the rolled strips in the steamer. Steam for 50 minutes. After expansion, unwrap the aluminum foil and store for consumption.

30. <u>Garbanzo Burgers</u>

Serving: 8 patties

Ingredients

- ❖ 3 tablespoons of sesame seeds
- ❖ 1/3 cup of potato flour
- ❖ 5 dashes of salt
- ❖ 3 dashes of cayenne pepper
- ❖ ¼ tablespoon of cardamom or coriander (grounded)
- ❖ ½ tablespoon of ground cumin
- ❖ 1 tablespoon of curry powder
- ❖ 3 teaspoons of soy sauce
- ❖ ¾ cup cooked brown rice
- ❖ 1 cup of garbanzo beans (cooked)
- ❖ 1 medium sized minced garlic clove
- ❖ 1-2 chopped celery stalks
- ❖ 2 small chopped carrots
- ❖ 2 small chopped onions
- ❖ Small amount of vegetable oil for spraying

Directions

1. Cook the sesame seeds in a pan until they start to pop. Grate the seeds using a food processor and add the carrot, onion, garlic, and celery.

2. Cut some beans using the pulse feature of a food processor leaving some chunks. Mix this to the vegetable mixture together with the brown rice, curry powder, cumin, soy sauce, cayenne, salt, and coriander. Mix well.

3.   Mix in some potato flour to have a firm dough. Knead for 1 minutes then form 8 patties.
4.   Grease a pan with vegetable oil spray. Cook the patties over medium-high heat for 5 minutes for one side and another 5 minutes for the other side.

31. <u>Vegan Spicy Asian Style Burgers</u>

Ingredients

- ❖ 1/3 cup of tamari
- ❖ 1 ½ cup of vegetable stock
- ❖ 1/3 cup of brown sugar
- ❖ 1 tablespoon of sesame oil
- ❖ ½ teaspoon of liquid smoke
- ❖ 1 ½ teaspoon of Worcestershire sauce
- ❖ 1 small sliced and peeled ginger
- ❖ 5 small smashed garlic cloves
- ❖ 1 small chopped yellow onion
- ❖ 3 Portobello mushrooms (clean)
- ❖ 1 ½ cup of frozen edamame
- ❖ 2 tablespoon of flax seed
- ❖ 3 teaspoons of mushroom powder
- ❖ 1 cup of breadcrumbs
- ❖ Small amount of olive oil for the pan
- ❖ ¾ cup of vegan mayo
- ❖ 5 teaspoons of gochujang
- ❖ 6 sesame seed buns
- ❖ 1 cup of drained and sliced kimchi
- ❖ 1 ½ cup of chopped romaine lettuce
- ❖ 1 medium-sized Asian pear (peeled and sliced)

Directions

1. Start by preheating the oven to 360 degrees Fahrenheit. Whisk brown sugar, tamari, liquid smoke, ginger, onion, garlic, stock, sesame oil, and Worcestershire sauce. Place the mushrooms in a casserole dish. Slowly pour the

whisked mixture over the mushrooms. Cover with aluminum foil and bake for 50 minutes. On the other hand, add edamame and pulse it using a food processor. Transfer to a mixing bowl. Set aside.

2. When the mushrooms are done cooking, let it cool. Remove excess liquid from the cooked mushroom and cut them. Extract the ginger, onion, garlic, from the cooking liquid. Reserve all ingredients.

3. Add the ginger, onions, mushrooms, and garlic in a food processor. Mix well. Combine the mushroom mixture with the chopped edamame, then fold is the mushroom powder, breadcrumbs, and flax mixture.

4. Now, split the mixture into 6 patties. Roll into a circular form then flatten. Garnish the top with olive oil and bake for 40 minutes. Meanwhile, add the reserved braising mixture in a small-sized pan over medium heat. Simmer the liquid until it is reduced to half. Whisk the brown sugar and simmer for about 4 minutes until it is dissolved. Let it cool. Set aside. Using a small-sized mixing bowl, add the gochujang and mayo, whisking together to combine.

5. Take the patties out from the oven. Brush one side of the baked patty with the brown sugar glaze. Place the patty, one that's glazed, in a grill pan over medium heat. Grill for about 5 minutes, garnishing the top with glaze, then grill the newly garnished side for another 5

minutes. Brush the top again with additional glaze.

6. Cook sesame seed buns and cut into half. Place mayo on one side and add the patty on the other side. Add kimchi, pear slices, and lettuce inside the bun. Serve.

32. Seitan Baked in Sweet and Sour Sauce

Ingredients

For the seitan

❖ 1 ½ cup of wheat gluten
❖ 6 teaspoons of nutritional yeast
❖ 1/8 tablespoon onion powder
❖ ½ cup water
❖ 5 teaspoons of peanut butter
❖ ½ teaspoon of sesame oil
❖ 3 teaspoons of soy sauce
❖ ¼ tablespoon of garlic (minced)
❖ ¼ tablespoon of ginger (minced)
❖ ¾ recipe of sweet and sour orange sauce

Directions

1. Preheat the oven to 360 degrees Fahrenheit and brush a baking dish with canola oil. Mix the wheat gluten, yeast, and onion powder in a large-sized mixing bowl. Add in the water with the sesame oil, peanut butter, ginger, soy sauce, and add it to the remaining dry ingredients. Mix well and knead.

2. Place the dough in a baking dish. Evenly flatten the dough in the baking dish. Using a sharp knife, cut the dough into 10 strips forming 20 strips.

3. Bake for about 25 minutes. Meanwhile, prepare the sauce needed. After 25 minutes, glaze the half of the sauce over the top covering the

seitan completely. Bake for another 15 minutes. Let it cool and then serve.

Sweet and Sour Orange Sauce

* ❖ ¾ teaspoon of minced garlic
* ❖ ¾ teaspoon of minced ginger
* ❖ ½ cup of orange juice
* ❖ ½ cup of white wine vinegar
* ❖ 6 teaspoons of tomato paste
* ❖ 9 teaspoons of brown sugar
* ❖ 6 teaspoons of agave nectar
* ❖ ¾ teaspoon of sesame oil
* ❖ 6 teaspoons of soy sauce
* ❖ 6 teaspoons of corn starch
* ❖ ¼ cup of vegetable broth

4. Grease the pan with canola oil and heat over medium heat. Place the ginger and garlic in the pan and cook for 3 minutes. Add the other ingredients except for broth and cornstarch.

5. Mix the remaining two ingredients until lump-free. Stir it together with the sauce. Keep warm.

For the vegetables

* ❖ 3 small wedge-chopped onions
* ❖ 2 teaspoons of minced garlic
* ❖ ¾ teaspoon of ginger paste
* ❖ Cauliflower head chopped into tiny florets
* ❖ 2 small strip-cut red bell pepper
* ❖ Half recipe of the Sweet and Sour Orange Sauce

Vegetable broth

6. Heat a large-sized pan over high heat. Sauté the onion. Add ginger paste and garlic and sauté for a minute.

7. Add a half cup of water and the cauliflower. Cover right away and steam for about 5 minutes. Add the bell pepper in the pan and cook for about 3-5 minutes.

8. Mix the sauce with the vegetables and use a small amount of vegetable broth to remove the sauce out of the pan. Stir and cook for about 8 minutes. Serve over noodles together with the seitan strips made.

33. Seitan Crimini Mushroom Roast

Ingredients

Wet ingredients

- ❖ 1.5 cup sliced crimini mushrooms
- ❖ 1 large minced garlic clove
- ❖ 2 cups of vegetable broth
- ❖ 2 tablespoons + 2 teaspoons of soy sauce
- ❖ 4 teaspoons of olive oil
- ❖ ¼ tablespoon of liquid smoke

Dry ingredients

- ❖ 2.3 cups of wheat gluten flour
- ❖ ½ cup of chickpea flour
- ❖ 2/3 cup of nutritional yeast
- ❖ 1 tablespoon of onion powder
- ❖ 1/8 tablespoon of dried thyme
- ❖ 1/8 tablespoon of dried sage
- ❖ 1/8 tablespoon of cumin
- ❖ 6 pinches of salt
- ❖ 3 pinches of salt

Directions

1. Heat up the oven to 380 degrees Fahrenheit.
2. Mix all the dry ingredients in a large bowl and set aside for a while.
3. Using the food mixer, pulse the mushrooms and garlic cloves into small pieces. Transfer it to a bowl and stir in the wet ingredients.

4. Mix the liquid into the dry ingredients and massage the dough to make a ball.

5. Get 2 pieces of 18 inches long aluminum foils and lay horizontally. Spray it with oil. Form the ball into a log about 12 inches.

6. Wrap the dough tightly and seal the ends.

7. Place them on the baking tray and bake for 50 minutes while rotating 4 times to ensure all sides are heated equally. It is already cooked once the dough is firm.

8. Let it stay for 8 minutes, then serve!

34. Barbecued "Ribs"

15 minutes to prepare
1 hour and 30 minutes to cook
A total of 1 hour and 45 minutes
16 strips or ribs

Ingredients

- ❖ 1.5 cup of wheat gluten
- ❖ 1 tablespoon of chipotle powder
- ❖ 1 tablespoon of lemon pepper
- ❖ 3 teaspoons of onion powder
- ❖ 3 teaspoons of garlic powder
- ❖ 1.5 cup of water
- ❖ 6 teaspoons of tahini
- ❖ 6 teaspoons of soy sauce

BBQ Sauce

- ❖ 1.5 cup of ketchup
- ❖ 1.5 cup of water
- ❖ ¼ cup of apple cider vinegar
- ❖ 1.5 tablespoon of brown sugar
- ❖ 1.5 tablespoon of white sugar
- ❖ 4 dashes of black pepper
- ❖ 3 teaspoons of onion powder
- ❖ 3 teaspoons of wet mustard
- ❖ ¼ tablespoon of dry mustard
- ❖ 2 teaspoons of lemon juice
- ❖ 3 teaspoons of Worcestershire sauce

Directions

1. Combine all the ingredients of the barbecue sauce in a saucepan, boil and simmer for an hour while frequently stirring.

2. Preheat the oven to 380 degrees Fahrenheit and grease a baking tray.

3. Take a large bowl and combine the first 5 dry ingredients.

4. Take out small bowl and combine the tahini, soy sauce, and water.

5. Add this to the dry ingredients and start kneading the dough until the mixture is combined.

6. Once done, lay the dough to the baking tray and cut 16 strips or "ribs".

7. Bake for 20 minutes while preparing to grill.

8. Remove the ribs and brush it with the barbecue sauce earlier.

9. Grill all the sides of the "ribs" until charred or browned.

10. Serve hot.

35. Quinoa Potato Cakes

25 minutes to prepare
35 minutes to cook
A total of 1 hour
4 servings

Ingredients

- ❖ 1.5 cup of cooked quinoa
- ❖ 3 medium sized boiled potatoes
- ❖ ¾ inch of crushed ginger
- ❖ ½ tablespoon of ground cumin
- ❖ 1.5 teaspoon of Garam Masala
- ❖ ¾ cup of fresh Coriander
- ❖ 3 chopped green chillies
- ❖ a little bit of salt
- ❖ olive oil for frying

Directions

1. Heat the quinoa based on the given instructions.
2. Mash the boiled potatoes.
3. In a large bowl, mix the mashed potatoes, quinoa, cumin, ginger, coriander, salt, jalapenos, garam masala, and some seasonings.
4. Create patties from the mixture.
5. Place 3 tablespoons of oil in a skillet and cook the patties until it gets the golden-brown color on both sides.
6. Once done, serve on a platter with a salad or with your favorite sauce!

36. __Chickpea and Rice Patties with Tahini Sauce__

Ingredients

For Patties

- ❖ 20 ounces of rinsed and drained garbanzo beans
- ❖ 1.5 cup of cooked brown rice
- ❖ 6 teaspoons red onions (chopped)
- ❖ 4 teaspoons minced garlic
- ❖ 6 teaspoons of fresh parsley (chopped)
- ❖ 6 teaspoons of fresh mint (chopped)
- ❖ ½ teaspoon of ground cumin
- ❖ 1.5 teaspoon of spike seasonings
- ❖ 4 pinches of salt
- ❖ 2 tablespoon of flaxseed
- ❖ 3-6 teaspoons of vegetable oil or grape seed

Yogurt-Tahini Sauce

- ❖ ½ cup of coconut yogurt
- ❖ 2 tablespoon of tahini sauce
- ❖ 1.5 tablespoon of lemon juice
- ❖ ½ teaspoon minced garlic
- ❖ ½ teaspoon of ground cumin
- ❖ ½ teaspoon of Sumac
- ❖ 1 to 3 tablespoons of water
- ❖ 2 dashes of salt

Directions

1. Combine all the ingredients of the yogurt – tahini sauce into a bowl. Once done, set it aside.

2. In a food mixer, mix the parsley, drained beans, red onion, mint, cumin, garlic, salt, spike seasoning, and 1 cup of rice. Finely chopped but don't over process.

3. Once done, place it in a bowl and add the flaxseed.

4. Scoop using a ¼ cup then flatten to make each patty. Refrigerate for 25 minutes to handle it easier later

5. Remove the patties from the fridge then cook the patties on a medium-low heat. Add the oil and cook until both sides are lightly brown.

6. Serve while hot and accompany with the yogurt-tahini sauce.

37.   **Apple & Sage Vegan Sausage**

Ingredients

- ❖   1.5 cup of dried apple
- ❖   2.5 cups of filtered water
- ❖   ¾ cup of oats
- ❖   ½ cup of wheat gluten
- ❖   2 tablespoons of nutritional yeast flakes
- ❖   1/8 cup of almond flour or meal
- ❖   ¾ cup of cooked brown rice
- ❖   3 teaspoons of ground flax seed
- ❖   6 dashes of sugar
- ❖   1.5 teaspoon of rubbed sage
- ❖   1.5 teaspoon of garlic powder
- ❖   1.5 teaspoon of lemon pepper
- ❖   ½ teaspoon of ground thyme
- ❖   ¼ teaspoon of ground cloves
- ❖   ¼ teaspoon of red pepper flakes (crushed)
- ❖   ¼ teaspoon of fennel seeds (crushed)
- ❖   5 pinches of salt
- ❖   5 teaspoons of liquid from the apples
- ❖   2 teaspoon of liquid smoke
- ❖   ¼ tablespoon of white rice vinegar

Directions

1.   On a saucepan, add water and place the apples. Cook over a high heat for 10 minutes. Spread the apples and let it cool. Don't throw the liquid for it will be used later.

2.   In a food mixer, pound the oats to break them into small pieces. Pour it into a bowl together with the pepper flakes, salt, fennel seeds,

cloves, thyme, lemon pepper, garlic powder, flaxseed, sage, sugar, brown rice, almond flour, yeast flakes, and wheat gluten.

3. Place the apples inside the food mixer and add vinegar, liquid smoke, and 2 tablespoons of the apple water. Mix for 3 minutes then add the non-wet ingredients from the bowl. Mix together. Once done return it to the bowl.

4. Preheat the oven to 350 degrees Fahrenheit.

5. In making the sausages, roll the dough to create a ball and stretch the dough. Make some 3-inch sausages and place them on the cookie sheet. Cover it with the aluminum foil and bake it for 15 minutes. Turn it to the other side and give it another 10 minutes.

6. Let it cool for 4 minutes then serve.

38. __White Bean Burgers__

Ingredients

- ❖ 20 ounces of rinsed and drained white beans
- ❖ 1/8 cup of diced onions
- ❖ 1 large sized minced garlic clove
- ❖ 1 small sized diced carrot
- ❖ ¾ cup oats
- ❖ 4 teaspoons of nutritional yeast
- ❖ 2 teaspoons of basil
- ❖ 6 dashes of pepper
- ❖ 4 dashes of chili powder
- ❖ ¼ teaspoon of garlic

Directions

1. Mix all ingredients in a blender or food mixer. Create 6 patties and bake them for 400 degrees Fahrenheit oven for 12 minutes on each side.

2. Note: if you want it to be garlicky, just add more garlic.

3. These burgers are best serve with quinoa pilaf.

39. <u>Quinoa Oregano Pilaf</u>

Ingredients

- ❖ ½ cup of quinoa
- ❖ ½ cup of water
- ❖ ½ cup of vegetable broth
- ❖ 2 teaspoons of olive oil
- ❖ ½ cup of diced onion
- ❖ 1 small diced carrot
- ❖ 3 small minced garlic cloves
- ❖ 3 teaspoons of nutritional yeast
- ❖ Pinches of pepper, oregano, basil, garlic, and salt

Directions

1. Sauté garlic, carrots, and onions on a medium – low heat for 7 minutes. Stir frequently.
2. Once the onions are a bit translucent, pour in the liquids, quinoa, and spices. Cover and cook until the liquid is absorbed.

40. <u>Homemade Delicious Tofu</u>

Ingredients

- ❖ 1 ½ lb of extra-firm tofu
- ❖ 1 cup of boiling water
- ❖ 1 ½ teaspoon of dill
- ❖ ¼ tablespoon of fresh rosemary
- ❖ ¼ tablespoon of dried thyme
- ❖ ¼ tablespoon of marjoram
- ❖ ¼ tablespoon of sage
- ❖ 7 dashes of black pepper
- ❖ 4 dashes of salt
- ❖ 3 medium sized minced garlic clove
- ❖ 1/3 cup of olive oil

Directions

1. Cut the tofu lengthwise to create 12 slices. Place on the baking tray and let it stay for a while.

2. Whip the garlic, olive oil and the spices on the 1 cup boiling water

3. Pour about a ¾ of the mixture on the tofu slices. Fridge them for 24 hours because the longer you marinate them, the more flavor the tofu has. Marinate every often.

4. Preheat the oven to 380 degrees Fahrenheit and pour the remaining marinade over the tofu. Bake it for 50 minutes. Once done, fry the slices until it gets a golden-brown color.

5. Serve the slices with your favorite foods!

6. Note: Can be refrigerated for 1 week inside a sealed container.

41. <u>Tempeh with Roasted Potatoes & Cauliflower</u>

Ingredients

Breaded Tempeh

- ❖ ¾ pack of soy tempeh
- ❖ 1.5 cup of apple juice
- ❖ 1.5 tablespoon of tamari
- ❖ 3 cups of flour
- ❖ 100 ml of vegan milk
- ❖ 5 cups of panko breadcrumbs
- ❖ 3 teaspoons of chopped parsley
- ❖ Pinches of salt and pepper

Directions

1. Chop the tempeh into half and cut it to 10 cutlets. After, steam some tamari and apple juice for 15 minutes. Let it cool.

2. Pour the following ingredients into different plates: flour, vegan milk, panko breadcrumbs with parsley, salt, and pepper.

3. Dip the tempeh with flour and then to the milk it and dip into the panko breadcrumbs. Using a pan, heat sunflower oil and cook the tempeh.

Mustard Roasted Pottoes

- ❖ 1 ½ lb of fingerling potatoes
- ❖ 1 small-sized onion
- ❖ 3 teaspoons of grainy Dijon mustard
- ❖ 6 teaspoons of olive oil
- ❖ Pinches of salt and pepper

4. Set the oven to 420 degrees Fahrenheit. Chop the potatoes in half. Then slice some onions. Using a large-sized mixing bowl, whisk the oil, mustard, salt, and pepper. Add the onions and potatoes and coat. Place the coated potatoes and onions on a baking sheet. Bake for about 50 minutes.

Mashed Cauliflower & Broccoli

❖   ¾ head cauliflower
❖   ½ medium-sized head of broccoli
❖   1 tablespoon of Earth Balance
❖   2 teaspoons of nutritional yeast

5. Separate the broccoli and cauliflower. Put them in a pot and fill half of the pot with water. Steam. Remove excess water and place a tablespoon of Earth Balance and about 1 ½ teaspoon of nutritional yeast. Puree the mixture using a potato masher. Plate it and serve.

42. <u>Vegan Pepperoni</u>

Ingredients

- ❖ 1.5 cups of wheat gluten
- ❖ 3 teaspoons of nutritional yeast
- ❖ ¾ cup of vegetable broth
- ❖ 2 teaspoons of liquid aminos

Seasoning Blend

- ❖ ½ tablespoon of paprika
- ❖ ½ tablespoon of ground mustard
- ❖ ¼ tablespoon of fennel
- ❖ ¼ tablespoon of dried oregano
- ❖ ¼ tablespoon of dried thyme leaves
- ❖ ¼ tablespoon of dried basil leaves
- ❖ ¼ tablespoon of onion powder
- ❖ ¼ tablespoon of garlic powder
- ❖ ½ teaspoon of ground anise seed
- ❖ ¼ teaspoon of cayenne pepper
- ❖ 4 dashes of salt
- ❖ 4 dashes of ground black pepper

Directions

1. Preheat the oven to 370 degrees Fahrenheit.
2. Mix all the ingredients in a large bowl and stir lightly.
3. Roll out the dough into small sausages.
4. Wrap them using an aluminum foil and place inside the oven. Bake for 30 to 50 minutes.

43. Lentil patties with roasted tomato sauce

Ingredients

* ❖ 300 grams of punnet cherry tomatoes cut into half
* ❖ ¼ cup of shredded basil
* ❖ 600 grams of sweet potato, peeled and chopped into pieces
* ❖ ¾ tablespoon of olive oil
* ❖ 2 small chopped onions
* ❖ 2 small crushed garlic cloves
* ❖ ¼ tablespoon of ground cumin
* ❖ ¼ tablespoon of ground coriander
* ❖ 1 kilogram can brown lentils, rinsed and drained
* ❖ ½ cup of breadcrumbs
* ❖ ½ cup of vegetable oil

Directions

1. Preheat the oven to 190 degrees Celsius. Cut the tomatoes on a tray and heat for 25 minutes. After heating, cool it for 12 minutes. Put it on a food mixer to create a chunky sauce. Add some pepper and basil and then mix.

2. Rinse the sweet potato. Cook until the potatoes are tender. Drain the water, transfer it to a bowl and mash using a fork.

3. Heat the oil in a pan on a low heat. Add the onions for 7 minutes. Stir in the cumin, coriander, garlic for 50 seconds.

4. Combine the onion mixture, lentils, pepper, salt, and sweet potato using a fork and form 8 burger patties. Cover both sides with breadcrumbs.

5. Heat the oil in a pan over low heat and cook the patties for 4 minutes on both sides. Once done, serve the patties with sauce on top. You can also put some basil.

44. <u>Vegan Chorizo</u>

Ingredients

- ❖ 1 ½ lb of extra-firm tofu, drained
- ❖ 4 medium-sized ancho peppers
- ❖ 2 medium-sized chopped garlic cloves
- ❖ 3 teaspoons of dried oregano
- ❖ 1 tablespoon of paprika
- ❖ 1 tablespoon of cumin seeds
- ❖ ½ tablespoon of salt
- ❖ 1.5 teaspoons of red pepper flakes
- ❖ 3 whole cloves
- ❖ 1.5 teaspoons of ground cinnamon
- ❖ 1/8 cup of apple cider vinegar
- ❖ 1.5 tablespoons of peanut butter
- ❖ 1.5 teaspoon of salt
- ❖ 2 teaspoons of olive oil
- ❖ 2 cups of vegetable stock

Directions

1. Rip the ancho peppers into pieces and roast in a skillet for 3 minutes or until you smell the aroma of it. Once done, mix it with the other ingredients except for the vegetable stock and tofu in a mixer. Beat to blend. Pour in the stock 1 cup at a time and pulse again to blend. Add the mashed tofu and the spice mixture. Cook it on a medium heat for 30-40 minutes while frequently stirring. Serve when done.

45. Easy Seitan

Ingredients

Broth

- ❖ 7 cups of water
- ❖ 5 teaspoons of dark molasses
- ❖ 4 tablespoons of soy sauce
- ❖ 1.5 tablespoon of fresh ginger (grated)

Dry mixture

- ❖ 1.5 cup of wheat gluten
- ❖ 4 tablespoons of chickpea flour
- ❖ 5 teaspoons of nutritional yeast flakes
- ❖ 6 dashes of garlic powder
- ❖ 6 dashes of onion powder
- ❖ 2.5 cups of cold water

Directions

1. Boil the broth ingredients in a pot.
2. While heating the broth, mix the remaining ingredients in a bowl. Knead with your hands until it becomes bouncy.
3. Place the dough on a parchment paper, divide into half and roll. Cut each roll into 32 pieces.
4. When the broth boils, drop some gluten pieces. Lower down the heat and let it simmer for an hour. Cool the seitan and divide it to serve 8 people. Place inside an airtight container and freeze if not all are eaten.

46. <u>Tofu Nut Balls</u>

24 tofu nut balls
10 minutes to prepare
25 minutes to cook
Total of 35 minutes

Ingredients

- ❖ 1.5 cup of breadcrumbs
- ❖ ¾ cup of whole pecans
- ❖ ¼ cup chopped onions
- ❖ 1/3 cup of quick oats
- ❖ 6 teaspoons of nutritional yeast flakes
- ❖ ¼ tablespoon of dried basil leaves
- ❖ ½ teaspoon of garlic powder
- ❖ 2 dashes of cayenne pepper
- ❖ 1 brick of tofu (crushed)
- ❖ 3 dashes of salt
- ❖ 2 teaspoons of soy sauce
- ❖ 4 tablespoons of water

Directions

1. Preheat the oven to 380 F
2. In a large bowl, mix all the ingredients
3. Create balls 24 balls and bake for 20-25 minutes or until the balls are golden brown.
4. Serve while still hot and top with basil or mozzarella if you like.

47.   <u>Vegan Potato Pecan Burgers</u>

4 servings

Ingredients

- ❖   1.5 cups of mashed sweet potatoes (peeled and cooked)
- ❖   1/3 cup of uncooked quinoa
- ❖   1 cup of water
- ❖   5 teaspoons of olive oil
- ❖   6 teaspoons of maple syrup
- ❖   2 dashes of cayenne pepper
- ❖   1/3 cup of chopped roasted pecans
- ❖   ¾ cup of chopped kale
- ❖   ¾ teaspoon of sea salt
- ❖   1 small sweet onion
- ❖   3 dashes of ground black pepper
- ❖   4 burger buns

Preparation

1.   Preheat the oven to 370 degrees Fahrenheit

2.   Heat the quinoa.

3.   On a pan, mix the cayenne pepper, 3 teaspoons of maple syrup and olive oil

4.   In this mixture, add the pecans, kale, sea salt, quinoa, and the mashed potatoes

5.   From this, make 4 patties and bake it for 25 minutes on each side.

6.   When the patties are almost done, chop the onion and heat the remaining 2 teaspoons of olive oil in a skillet.

7. Cook the onion and add the grounded black pepper and sea salt. (10 minutes)
8. Lower the heat and add the remaining 3 teaspoons of maple syrup. Stir and cook for 2 more minutes.
9. Once done, pour the mixture on top of the baked burgers.

48.   Veggie Burgers

Ingredients

- ❖ 15 ounces of rinsed and drained kidney beans
- ❖ 15 ounces of rinsed and drained chickpeas
- ❖ 1 small chopped onion
- ❖ 1 small chopped red bell pepper
- ❖ 2 chopped celery stalks
- ❖ ½ teaspoon minced jar garlic
- ❖ 2 cups cooked broccoli
- ❖ 3 teaspoons of Bragg liquid aminos
- ❖ 1/3 cup of cooked quinoa
- ❖ ½ ground of flax seed
- ❖ 1.5 teaspoon of ground cumin
- ❖ 1 teaspoon of ground sage
- ❖ 2 teaspoons of parsley flakes (dried)
- ❖ 2 teaspoon of cilantro flakes (dried)
- ❖ ½ teaspoon of ground thyme

Directions

1. Crush beans in a large bowl and mix all the ingredients.
2. Create your desired size for the patties and cook for 25 minutes on a medium heat.
3. If you want to bake, bake them in the oven at 400 degrees Fahrenheit for 15-20 minutes.

49. <u>Nutty Veggie Burger</u>

Ingredients

- ❖ 1/3 cup diced onion
- ❖ 2 small minced garlic cloves
- ❖ 3 tablespoons ground flax mixed with 1/3 cup of warm water
- ❖ ¾ cup oat flour
- ❖ 1 cup breadcrumbs
- ❖ 2 medium sized grated carrots
- ❖ 1.5 cup mashed black beans (cooked)
- ❖ ½ cup chopped almonds
- ❖ 1/3 cup sunflower seeds
- ❖ 3 teaspoons olive oil
- ❖ 2 teaspoons tamari
- ❖ 1 teaspoon chili powder
- ❖ 1.5 teaspoon cumin
- ❖ 1.5 teaspoon oregano
- ❖ 6 dashes of black pepper and kosher salt

Makes 4 Patties

- ❖ ½ cup minced onion
- ❖ 2 small minced garlic cloves
- ❖ Flax recipe
- ❖ 1 cup of oat flour
- ❖ 1 cup of breadcrumbs
- ❖ ¾ cup of grated carrots
- ❖ 1 cup of rinsed and drained cooked black beans
- ❖ 6 teaspoons of chopped parsley
- ❖ 8 teaspoons of chopped almonds
- ❖ ½ cup of sunflower seeds
- ❖ 2 teaspoons of extra virgin olive oil

- ❖ 2 teaspoons of tamari
- ❖ 1 teaspoon of chili powder
- ❖ ¾ teaspoon of cumin
- ❖ ¾ teaspoon of oregano
- ❖ ¾ teaspoon of Kosher salt and pepper

Directions

1. On a large pan, cook the garlic and onions with 1.5 teaspoons of oil. After cooking, mix together with the flax seed in a bowl. Set aside for 11 minutes.

2. Add the remaining ingredients except for the salt and spices and stir well. After mixing, add salt and seasonings.

3. With damp hands, shape the mixture into burger patties.

4. Frying: add a little oil to the pan and cook the burgers on each side for 6 minutes on a medium-low heat.

5. Baking: Heat the oven to 400 degrees Fahrenheit and bake the burgers on each side for 12 minutes.

6. Barbecue: Pre-bake first the burgers for 10 minutes before grilling them.

50. __Black Bean & Quinoa Veggie Burgers__

Ingredients

Patties

- ❖ 1/3 cup of dry quinoa
- ❖ 2 teaspoons of olive oil
- ❖ 1 small chopped onion
- ❖ 2 medium sized minced garlic cloves
- ❖ 1 tablespoon of kosher salt
- ❖ Small can of black beans
- ❖ 5 teaspoons of tomato paste
- ❖ 2 tablespoons of flax seed
- ❖ ½ cup of frozen corn
- ❖ 1/3 cup of chopped cilantro
- ❖ 2 minced chipotle in adobo
- ❖ 2.5 teaspoon of ground cumin
- ❖ 1/3 cup of rolled oats
- ❖ ½ cup of oat flour

Yogurt Sauce

- ❖ 1/3 cup of Greek yogurt (fat free)
- ❖ 3 teaspoons of honey
- ❖ 2 teaspoons of Dijon mustard

Directions

1. Apply a medium-low heat on a saucepan with a mixture of a cup of water and quinoa and then boil. Lower the heat, cover and cook until the quinoa is cooked. Set aside.

2. On a heated pan, add the salt, garlic, and onion and cook it for 4-5 minutes. Put the mixture in a bowl and add the black beans. Use a potato masher or if not a fork and mash the mixture until pastry mixture is created.

3. Add the flax seed, tomato paste, cilantro, corn, cumin, remaining salt, chipotles, oat flour, oats, and cooked quinoa. Mix them well. Form 6 burger patties and place them on the baking sheet. Use a plastic wrapper to cover them and refrigerate for a few hours.

4. For your yogurt sauce, combine the honey, mustard, and yogurt in a small container.

5. Heat the oven for 370 degrees Fahrenheit. Take out a baking sheet and spray it with cooking spray. Put the made patties on the baking sheet and bake if for 11 minutes. Flip them over and give it another 9 minutes. Once done, serve them with some yogurt sauce.

51. <u>Spicy Sausage</u>

Ingredients

- ❖ 20 ounces of rinsed, drained, and mashed cannellini beans
- ❖ 3 teaspoons of tomato paste
- ❖ ¾ cup of water
- ❖ 2 teaspoons of olive oil
- ❖ 2.5 tablespoon of soy sauce
- ❖ 1 large minced garlic clove
- ❖ 1 cup of wheat gluten
- ❖ 1/3 cup of nutritional yeast
- ❖ 1.5 teaspoon of Chinese red pepper flakes
- ❖ ¼ tablespoon of smoke
- ❖ ¼ tablespoon of dried oregano
- ❖ ¼ teaspoon of ground black pepper
- ❖ ¾ teaspoon of liquid smoke

Directions

1. With the finished sausages, sauté the sliced potatoes and onion in a small amount of oil. When it's time for the vegetables to get tender, add the seitan and cook it until it gets the color brown. After, add the pepper on top.

52.   <u>Quinoa Veggie Meatballs</u>

25 minutes to prepare
23 minutes cooking time
48 minutes total time
4 servings

Ingredients

* ❖   1.5 cup of cooked quinoa
* ❖   3 teaspoons of olive oil
* ❖   ½ cup chopped onions
* ❖   2 medium sized minced garlic cloves
* ❖   ¾ cup of diced zucchini
* ❖   1.5 teaspoon of dried oregano
* ❖   1.5 tablespoon of tomato paste
* ❖   1 tablespoon of flax seed
* ❖   ¼ cup of breadcrumbs

Directions

1.   Place a parchment paper on the baking sheet while preheating the oven to 370 degrees Fahrenheit.

2.   On a medium-low heat the oil and add garlic and onions for 6-7 minutes until softened.

3.   Add the tomato paste, pepper, oregano, zucchini and salt for 3-4 minutes.

4.   In a bowl of quinoa, add the whole wheat, breadcrumbs, and flax seed then stir. Add pepper or salt to add flavor.

5.   Roll meatballs about a round of tablespoon and put it on the baking sheet.

6. Bake each side for 10 minutes.

53. <u>Vegan Roast</u>

Ingredients

Roast

- ❖ 1 teaspoon of garlic powder
- ❖ 1 1/2 cups water
- ❖ 2 teaspoons of onion powder
- ❖ 12 oz firm tofu
- ❖ 1/2 cup soy
- ❖ 1/2 cup nutritional yeast
- ❖ 3 tablespoons of soy sauce
- ❖ 1 tablespoon olive oil
- ❖ 2 cups wheat gluten

Broth: (1 1/2 amount of broth should be used while stuffing the roast)

- ❖ 1 teaspoon each of them, freshly chopped sage, thyme and rosemary
- ❖ 2 tablespoons olive oil
- ❖ 4 cloves minced garlic
- ❖ 2 1/3 cups of vegetable broth

Direction

1. Oven should be preheated to 325 F.
2. Mix the dry elements in a mixing bowl.
3. Tofu, water, soy sauce and olive oil should be added to a food processor and blended until combined.
4. The dry mixtures are next to add to the food processor.
5. Ball form will be made in the mixture.

6. In case of not stuffing, place them in a baking pan after form into two loaves

7. While stuffing, the dough has to be divided in half.

8. Roll out the half part on a clean plate using a wet rolling pin. 15" circle is the right shape.

9. Make a pile by 3 1/2 cups stuffing in the middle.

10. Now the dough can be folded up around the stuffing into a shape of loaf, while pinching to seal. Same thing should be done with the second half of the dough and placed the loaves into a baking pan.

11. Then 1/2 cup of broth has to be poured over the top of the roasts and the pan should be covered with foil. The foil has to be removed after baking for 30 minutes. Then add half of the remaining broth and again bake for another 30 minutes, occasionally basting. After that remove the pan from the oven to flip the loaves over. Then pour the remaining broth over the loaves and again bake for another 30 minutes, basting occasionally.

12. By the end of the cooking time, the roasts should completely soak up the broth. If they don't, just keep cooking in 30 minute increments, until there is little or no broth left ,basting every 10 minutes or so.

13. Remove the roasts from the pans, let it cool for at least 5 minutes then slice it up and serve.

54. Sweet Potato Avocado Veggie Burger

Ingredients

- ❖ Medium sweet potato, peeled and baked -1
- ❖ White beans canned, drained, rinsed and cooked -16 oz.
- ❖ White onion, chopped-1/2 cup
- ❖ Tahina-2-3 Tbsp
- ❖ Apple cider vinegar-3/4 tsp
- ❖ Garlic powder-1 tsp
- ❖ Chipotle powder -1/2 - 1 tsp
- ❖ Salt-1/2 tsp
- ❖ Black pepper -1/4 tsp
- ❖ Nutritional yeast -1/3 cup
- ❖ Finely chopped greens (like kale, spinach, parsley) -1/2 - 1 cup
- ❖ Avocado, tomato, burger buns, vegenaise, greens for toppings
- ❖ Virgin coconut oil, Skillet :1 Tbsp

Directions

1. Bake for 40-60 minutes the sweet potato in a oven heated 400 degree until tender. In a hurry, the microwave can be used to do it fast.

2. In a large mixing bowl, add the potato and beans. Mash well using a large fork. Keep mashing after folding in the onion. Then after adding other remaining burger elements keep mashing until it gets thickened. Before adding

to bowl you can rinse the beans in warm water which makes them easier to be mashed.

3. The oven should be heated 400 degrees.

4. Add the coconut oil after heating a skillet on high heat.

5. After forming the burger combination to large patties they should be placed on the very warm skillet. To brown them, cook 1 to 3 minutes on both sides. Now try all the steps again with all the mixture and make at least 8 small or 6 large patties.

6. After cooking on skillet, place the patties on a baking sheet then bake for about 10-15 minutes, till they are cooked through.

7. While toasting the buns, slice up all the burger toppings. You can add vegan mayo on the patty and toppings. These must be served warm.

8. You can store the leftover burgers, in fridge for a certain day, sealed. These can also be frozen and eaten within some weeks for best taste and texture. To reheat: depending on burger thickness, heat in a 400 degree oven till warmed through, for 12 minutes.

55. <u>Seitan Grilled Brisket</u>

Ingredients

- ❖ ¼ cups soy sauce
- ❖ 4 cloves garlic fine minced
- ❖ 3 tablespoons date paste
- ❖ 1 cups marsala wine
- ❖ 2 ½ cups vegetable stock
- ❖ ½ cups tomato paste
- ❖ ½ tablespoon chipotle powder
- ❖ 3 1/2 cups of vital wheat gluten flour
- ❖ 2 tablespoons onion powder
- ❖ ¼ cups nutritional yeast
- ❖ 1 tablespoon garlic powder

Directions

1. Preheat oven to 375 degrees F.
2. In a small bowl combine the minced garlic, soy sauce, date paste, marsala win and tomato paste. Mix well and add the vegetable stock. Mix well.
3. In another large bowl add the yeast with the flour.
4. Add the garlic and onion powder.
5. Add half the soy sauce mixture to the flour mixture.
6. Knead into dough and create loaf into 2 inch thick loaves.
7. Arrange the loaves onto baking tray.

8. Brush the soy sauce mixture on top and bake in the oven for about 30 minutes.
9. Brush the soy sauce again and bake for another 30 minutes. Serve warm.

56.   Mushroom Loaf Masala

Ingredients

- ❖ 12 small crimini mushrooms, minced
- ❖ 7 oz extra firm tofu, crumbled
- ❖ 1 tablespoon olive oil
- ❖ 1/2 small red onion, minced
- ❖ 1.5 tablespoons garam masala, toasted
- ❖ 1 bird's eye chili, minced
- ❖ 2 tsp brown sugar
- ❖ 8 dried curry leaves, crushed
- ❖ 2 tablespoons melted EB
- ❖ 1/2 red pepper, minced
- ❖ 2/3 cup mashed potato
- ❖ 1 tsp fennel seeds
- ❖ 1 tablespoon nutritional yeast
- ❖ 1/2 tsp turmeric
- ❖ 2/3 cup raw cashew pieces
- ❖ 1/2 tsp asofoetida
- ❖ 1 tablespoon sea salt
- ❖ 1 tablespoon flax meal
- ❖ Canola oil, to coat

Directions

1. Preheat the oven to 350 degrees F.
2. Arrange parchment paper onto the loaf pan and coat with canola oil.
3. In a skillet heat the olive oil and fry the onion and pepper.
4. Add the mushrooms and fry for 10 minutes.

5. Transfer the mushroom mix onto a plate and cover with a lid.
6. Make paste of the cashews in a blender.
7. Combine the cashew paste with the mushroom. Add the rest of the ingredients one by one.
8. Add them to the loaf pan. Cover the top using aluminum foil.
9. Bake in the preheated oven for about 50 minutes.
10. Remove the aluminum foil and bake for another 20 minutes and serve warm.

57.   Lentil & Super-Grain Cutlets

Ingredients

- ❖ Quinoa, rinsed many times and drained-1/2 cup
- ❖ Red lentils and rinsed-3/4 cup
- ❖ Medium onion, nicely minced-1/2
- ❖ Cloves of garlic, pressed- 3-4
- ❖ Rosemary, crushed-1/2 teaspoon
- ❖ Black pepper, freshly ground-1/4 teaspoon
- ❖ Poultry seasoning -1 teaspoon
- ❖ Thyme-1 teaspoon
- ❖ Nutritional yeast-1 tablespoon
- ❖ Celery salt-1/2 teaspoon
- ❖ Salt-1 teaspoon
- ❖ Smoked paprika-1 teaspoon
- ❖ Vital wheat gluten-3/4 cup

Directions

1. Till the lentils are tender, cook the quinoa and lentils in 4 cups of water, for 20 minutes. Move from heat and let it cool slightly.

2. Lightly oil a baking sheet after preheating the oven to 350F.

3. When you understand you can handle the quinoa/lentil mixture after it has cooled enough, pour the mixture into a large bowl after draining the excess water. Stir well after adding all the remaining ingredients but the gluten. Add the gluten and gently knead the dough with hands for 5 minutes, to make the gluten developed.

4. Divide the dough into half pieces; then divide all of them in half again. Keep dividing them till you are left with 8 pieces. Shape them into rectangles after flattening them so that they're 1/2-3/4-inch thick. Now keep them within baking sheet and bake 20 minutes. Bake for another 10-15 minutes after turning each one over. Try not to overcook them, otherwise they will be dry.. Now you can enjoy them with your favorite taste of gravy.

58. <u>Herb Infused Cauliflower Falafel</u>

Ingredients

- ❖ Flax meal-2 tablespoons
- ❖ Boiling water -6 tablespoons
- ❖ Cauliflower florets-1 cup
- ❖ Carrots, chopped into thick solid pieces -1 cup
- ❖ Red onion-1 small piece
- ❖ garlic clove -1 piece
- ❖ Fresh parsley leaves-1 cup
- ❖ Lemon juice, freshly squeezed-1 tablespoon
- ❖ Ground cumin-1 1/2 teaspoons
- ❖ Sea salt-1 teaspoon
- ❖ Cayenne pepper - 1/2 teaspoon
- ❖ Sesame seeds-1 tablespoon
- ❖ Pumpkin seeds-1 tablespoon
- ❖ Almond meal-1/2 cup
- ❖ Olive oil – To fry

Directions

1. Combine flax seed including boiling water in a little bowl then stir till nicely combined. Wait for a few minutes to be thick.

2. Mix cauliflower, carrots, onion, garlic and parsley in a food processor. Keep pulsing till all are chopped coarsely. Pulse again adding lemon juice, cayenne, cumin, and salt. By now, the mixture should be very nicely chopped.

3. Knead until mixture holds together after transferring mixture to a bowl. And then add

flax seed mixture with almond meal. You can add more almond meal if the mixture seems to be wet. After that sesame and pumpkin seeds should be added.

4. With the palm of your hand ,form them into patties size. About 6 patties should be made from the batter.

5. Cook patties over medium heat for 3-4 minutes on each side, after coating a frying pan with olive oil. Let them become lightly browned.

6. Serving must be immediate. With a fresh salad or coconut yogurt dip, they will taste the best.

59. Sloppy Joe with Coconut Spinach

Ingredients

For the Sloppy Joe

- ❖ 1 pound seitan, chopped
- ❖ 1 tablespoon coconut oil
- ❖ 1 tablespoon fresh lime juice
- ❖ 1 medium onion, diced
- ❖ 3 cloves garlic, minced
- ❖ 14 oz can crushed tomatoes
- ❖ 1 tablespoon minced fresh ginger
- ❖ 1/2 teaspoon allspice
- ❖ 1 tablespoon sweet paprika
- ❖ 1/8 teaspoon cinnamon
- ❖ 1/2 teaspoon salt
- ❖ black pepper to taste
- ❖ 2 tablespoon pure maple syrup
- ❖ 1/2 teaspoon red pepper flakes
- ❖ 2 tablespoons chopped fresh thyme
- ❖ 2 teaspoons yellow mustard

For the spinach

- ❖ 2 cloves minced garlic
- ❖ 1 cup coconut milk
- ❖ 1 lb spinach
- ❖ 2 star anise
- ❖ 2 teaspoons coconut oil
- ❖ 1/4 teaspoon salt

Directions

Prepare the Sloppy Joe:

1. In a pan heat half the oil and fry the onion for 3 minutes.
2. Add in the seitan and toss for 10 minutes.
3. Add in the ginger, garlic and the rest of the oil.
4. Add the cinnamon, paprika, black pepper, salt, red pepper flakes and allspice.
5. Toss for 2 minutes and add in the tomatoes. Cook for 10 minutes.
6. Add in the lime juice, mustard and maple syrup and season using salt. Toss for another 5 minutes and take off the heat.

Prepare the spinach

7. In a skillet heat the oil and fry the garlic for 1 minute.
8. Add the spinach and toss for just 20 seconds or so.
9. Take off the heat and squeeze out the extra liquid.
10. Add the spinach back to the skillet and add the remaining ingredients.
11. Cook for about 15 minutes and serve with the sloppy Joe.

60. **Black Bean Tex-Mex Burgers**

Ingredients

Burgers

- ❖ black beans, canned but unsalted- 1 1/2 cups
- ❖ Fine bread crumbs-3 Tbsp
- ❖ Baked sweet potato-3/4 cup
- ❖ Chopped cilantro with stems-3 Tbsp
- ❖ Diced white onion- 1/3 cup
- ❖ Garlic powder - 1 tsp
- ❖ Chopped garlic-1 tsp
- ❖ Salt- 3/4 tsp
- ❖ Black pepper-1 tsp
- ❖ Olive oil-2 Tbsp
- ❖ Cider vinegar-1 Tbsp
- ❖ Lime juice-2 Tbsp
- ❖ Jalapeno, diced-1/2
- ❖ Nutritional yeast - 3 Tbsp
- ❖ Chipotle powder - A few dashes

Special Spicy Sauce

- ❖ Vegan mayo-1/2 cup
- ❖ Garlic hot sauce-2 tsp
- ❖ Onion tomato slices-5 round each
- ❖ Optional: lime-avocado slices with lemon juice spritzed

Directions

1. At first, prepare the Fiesta Slaw following the recipe – Cool it in fridge till it gets ready to be added to the burgers.

2. Spicy sauce should be whipped up after that and then set aside in fridge like former step.

3. Next step is preparing the burgers. Take a food processor and pulse all the ingredients in it. Hands can be used to mash them up. Next, place the burger patties on a lightly greased baking sheet after hand-forming them with the mixture.

4. Bake the burgers for 30 minutes at 375 degrees. Let it cool for some minutes till you assemble the burgers. Add your burger buns to the oven to toast them.

5. Now assemble the burgers. Get the bun warm, now spread of special sauce, optional avocado, onion, burger, fiesta slaw, tomato. You can add more slather of the special spicy sauce on the top of your bun according to your taste bud.

61. **Balsamic Wine Herb Seitan**

Ingredients

Seitan

- ❖ 8 ounce Seitan, sliced
- ❖ Fresh thyme (optional) 0.125 tsp
- ❖ Freshly ground pepper and salt
- ❖ Red wine 0.25 cup
- ❖ Balsamic vinegar 0.25 cup
- ❖ To taste 1 pinch
- ❖ Dried thyme 0.125 tsp
- ❖ Dried rosemary 0.125 tsp

Directions

1. Combine all the ingredients except the seitan.

2. Mix well and add the seitan in it.

3. Let it marinate for about 1 hour or longer.

4. In a pan add the seitan with its juice.

5. Cover and cook on low heat for about 10 minutes.

6. Flip it and cook for another 10 minutes.

7. Serve hot.

62. Black Bean Burger Patties With Pineapple

Ingredients

Guacamole

- ❖ 1/2 a jalapeno, minced
- ❖ 1 avocado, peeled and diced
- ❖ 1/4 cup cilantro, chopped
- ❖ 1/2 cup diced fresh pineapple
- ❖ 1 small shallot, minced
- ❖ 1 roasted hatch chile, chopped
- ❖ 1 tbsp fresh lime juice

Patties

- ❖ 1/4 onion, chopped
- ❖ 1/2 tablespoon flax seeds, ground
- ❖ 1/4 cup cilantro, chopped
- ❖ 1/3 cup cornmeal
- ❖ 1 garlic clove, roughly chopped
- ❖ 1 tsp ground cumin
- ❖ 1/2 of the jalapeno, roughly chopped
- ❖ 1 can black beans, rinsed

Directions

1. Soak the flax with water for 10 minutes.
2. In a mixing bowl combine the shallot, pineapple, lime juice, chile, cilantro, avocado and jalapeno and mix well.
3. For the patties, blend the onion, jalapeno, garlic, cumin, cilantro and blend until mixed.
4. Add the black beans, cornmeal and mix well.

5. Transfer to a bowl and add the flax mix.
6. Season using salt and pepper and mix well. Create flat patties using hands.
7. Fry the patties golden brown with oil and serve with the guacamole.

63. <u>Seitan Pot Roast</u>

Ingredients

For the Seitan

Dry mix

- ❖ 1 tablespoon tarragon, rubbed
- ❖ 2 tablespoons veggie bouillion powder
- ❖ 3 cups vital wheat gluten
- ❖ 1/4 cup soy flour
- ❖ Tons of freshly ground black pepper
- ❖ 1 tablespoon smoked salt
- ❖ 2 tablespoons fennel seed
- ❖ 1/4 cup nutritional yeast
- ❖ Fresh nutmeg, a couple rasps
- ❖ 1/2 cup tapioca flour

Wet mix

- ❖ 2 tablespoons tamari
- ❖ 1/3 cup olive oil
- ❖ 6 cloves garlic, minced
- ❖ 2/3 cup water
- ❖ 2 tablespoons smoke flavor
- ❖ 1 tablespoon honey

Directions

1. In a mixing bowl combine all the wet mix ingredients and mix well.
2. Combine all the dry ingredients in another mixing bowl.
3. Combine the both mixtures and create dough. Cover with cloth and set aside for now.

Accompanying Veggies

- ❖ 1 pound small carrots
- ❖ 1 package pearl onions, peeled
- ❖ 12 garlic cloves, peeled
- ❖ 1 small head raddichio, chopped
- ❖ 1 package baby bella mushrooms
- ❖ 1 package tiny potatoes
- ❖ 1/2 package grape tomatoes
- ❖ 1/4 fennel bulb, chopped

4. In a large pot add the fennel bulb following by the mushrooms, tomatoes, potatoes, garlic, onions, raddicio and carrots.

For braising the seitan

- ❖ 3/4 fennel bulb, chopped
- ❖ 4 tablespoons olive oil
- ❖ 2 tablespoons sun-dried tomatoes, chopped
- ❖ 2 tablespoons honey
- ❖ Fresh thyme, a sprig
- ❖ 2 stalks celery, chopped
- ❖ 1/2 package grape tomatoes, chopped
- ❖ Dash soy sauce
- ❖ 4 cups well-seasoned vegetable stock
- ❖ Dash hickory flavoring
- ❖ 4 cloves garlic, minced
- ❖ 1 cup bourbon

5. In a pot, fry the garlic with olive oil for a minute.

6. Add in the tomatoes, fennel, and celery. Toss for 5 minutes.

7. Stir in the remaining ingredients. Bring the mix to boil.

8. Turn the heat to low and simmer for 20 minutes.
9. Add this broth to the roasting pan on top of the veggies.
10. Roast for 4 hours.

Finishing touches

- ❖ 1/2 cup flour
- ❖ Canola oil
- ❖ Fresh black pepper, ground

11. Let the roast cool down and cut into slices of your choice.
12. In a skillet heat the oil and toss the flour for a minute or so.
13. Add on top of the roast and serve.

64. <u>Chickpea Filets With Aioli</u>

Ingredients

- ❖ 3 cups cooked chickpeas
- ❖ 1/2 tsp. marjoram
- ❖ 1 cup cooked brown rice
- ❖ 2 TBL Olive oil
- ❖ ½ tsp. basil
- ❖ ½ cup GF breadcrumbs
- ❖ 2 garlic cloves, minced
- ❖ ½ tsp. onion powder
- ❖ 5 scallions, sliced
- ❖ ½ tsp. mustard powder
- ❖ ½ tsp. oregano
- ❖ 1 tbsp soy sauce
- ❖ 1 tsp. thyme
- ❖ ½ tsp. garlic powder
- ❖ 1 yellow onion, diced
- ❖ ¼ tsp. lemon zest, optional

Directions

1. In a skillet heat the oil and fry the scallions with onion.
2. Add the garlic, marjoram, basil, oregano, and thyme.
3. Toss for 5 minutes and transfer to a bowl.
4. Add the brown rice with chickpeas in a blender and blend until smooth.
5. Add the garlic mix and blend again.
6. Transfer to a large mixing bowl and add the rest of the ingredients and mix well.

7. Create dough. Create filets and arrange on your baking tray.
8. Bake in the oven for 20 minutes with 400 degrees F.

Lemon dill aioli dipping sauce

- ❖ 1 tbsp freshly chopped Dill
- ❖ 1 tsp apple cider vinegar
- ❖ 1/4 c. Vegenaise Grapeseed
- ❖ 1 tsp lemon zest
- ❖ 1-2 tbsp lemon juice
- ❖ 1 clove garlic, finely minced

Directions

9. Combine all the sauce ingredients in a bowl.
10. Mix well and add on top of the filets.

65. **Legume Sweet Potato Burger**

Ingredients

- ❖ 1 1/4 cups dried chickpeas
- ❖ 1/4 teaspoon baking powder
- ❖ 3 tablespoons tahini
- ❖ 1/2 small red onion, sliced
- ❖ 1/4 cup chopped fresh dill
- ❖ 1/4 teaspoon black pepper
- ❖ 1 small orange sweet potato, grated
- ❖ 1 teaspoon kosher salt
- ❖ 1 medium cucumber, thinly sliced
- ❖ Olive oil cooking spray
- ❖ 2 tablespoons rice vinegar

Directions

1. Soak the chickpeas with 4 cups of water for about 24 hours.
2. Drain and set aside.
3. Preheat the oven to 375 degree F.
4. Add the chickpeas, black pepper, tahini, baking powder and a pinch of salt in a blender.
5. Blend for 2 minutes or until smooth.
6. Transfer to a large mixing bowl.
7. Add in the grated sweet potatoes, onion, vinegar, dill and mix well.
8. Create flat patties using hands.
9. Arrange onto a greased baking tray and bake in the oven for 20 minutes or so.

10. Flip the patties and bake for another 10 minutes.

11. Serve hot with dilly cucumbers.

66. **Plant Inspired Hungarian Goulash**

Ingredients

- ❖ 1 raw seitan recipe (below)
- ❖ 4 cups vegetable broth
- ❖ 2 tbsp olive oil
- ❖ 1/4 cup soy sauce
- ❖ 2 bay leaves
- ❖ 1 recipe Hungarian braised mushrooms, below
- ❖ 2 cups red wine substitute
- ❖ Salt and pepper to taste

Directions

1. In a skillet heat the oil and add the seitan. Season using salt and pepper.

2. Toss the seitan until it becomes brown.

3. Pour in the wine substitute and broth. Stir well.

4. Add the bay leaves, soy sauce and bring the mix to boil.

5. Turn the heat to low and simmer for about 1 hour.

Basic Seitan

- ❖ 2 tbsp soy sauce
- ❖ 2 cups vital wheat gluten
- ❖ 1 1/4 cup vegetable broth
- ❖ 1/2 cup all purpose flour
- ❖ several dashes of liquid smoke

6. Combine the all purpose flour, wheat gluten in a mixing bowl.

7. Add in the liquid smoke, broth and soy sauce.

8. Mix well and create dough.

9. Cut it into medium pieces.

67. Eastern European Braised Mushrooms

Ingredients

- ❖ 1 large sweet onion, thinly sliced
- ❖ 3 quarts button mushrooms
- ❖ 1 tbsp apple cider vinegar
- ❖ 2 red bell peppers, thinly sliced
- ❖ 2 tbsp olive oil
- ❖ 1 tbsp paprika
- ❖ 1/4 cup all purpose flour
- ❖ 3 tbsp soy sauce
- ❖ 1/4 cup tomato paste
- ❖ 1/4 tsp cayenne
- ❖ 4 cups vegetable stock
- ❖ 1/2 cup cashews
- ❖ 4 cloves garlic, minced
- ❖ 3/4 cup water

Directions

1. Fry the onion with oil for 3 minutes in a stock pot.
2. Add in the red peppers, garlic and mushroom. Toss for 8 minutes.
3. Add in the tomato paste, cayenne, paprika and flour.
4. Add in the broth and cover. Cook to bring it to boil.
5. Make a cashew paste in a blender with water and add to the pot.
6. Add the mushroom and apple cider vinegar.

68. "Chicken" Fried Steak

Ingredients

- ❖ 4 cups vital wheat gluten flour
- ❖ Spike seasoning to taste
- ❖ 1/2 cup nutritional yeast
- ❖ onion powder to taste
- ❖ 4 Tb flour
- ❖ 2 cups cold water
- ❖ tomato paste to taste
- ❖ 1 cup Bragg's liquid aminos
- ❖ fresh minced garlic to taste
- ❖ 2 Tb olive oil
- ❖ fresh chopped parsley

Directions

1. In a bowl combine the gluten flour with yeast and flour.
2. In another bowl combine the liquid aminos, cold water, and mix well.
3. Knead well and add all the rest of the ingredients.
4. Create dough and create medium buns.

Vegan Vegetable Broth

5. In a pot add the seitan pieces with the broth.
6. Bring to boil over high heat and simmer for 1 hour.
7. Take out the seitan onto a plate and reserve the broth.

Vegan Chicken Fried Steak Recipe

8.   In three different bowls, add flour in one, add soy milk, and squirts.

9.   In the third bowl mix crackers with spices of your choice.

10. Take the chicken patties and roll them onto the flour, then onto the soy milk mix and finally onto the crackers.

11. In a pan fry the patties golden brown and serve.

69. <u>Mushroom Mince Meat</u>

Ingredients

- ❖ Champignon mushrooms-250 grams
- ❖ Neutral oil -2 tablespoon
- ❖ Water-125 ml
- ❖ Salt and black pepper – For Tasting
- ❖ Button mushrooms-8.8 ounces

Directions

1. Grate or chop the mushrooms into very small pieces.

2. Turn the skillet on medium-high heat after placing the oil in it. Add the grated mushrooms and stir, once the oil is warm. Cook it for 5 minutes, then the mushrooms will begin to wilt.

3. Add the water after the mushrooms begin to wilt. Cook the mushrooms for 10-12 minutes more so that all the water has evaporated .By this the mushrooms will become completely soft.

4. After that mix salt and black pepper with the mushrooms .Let it cool for a while. Mince meat using the mushroom mixture like it is used in dishes such as Shepherd's Pie.

70. BBQ Seitan and Tempeh Southern Ribs

Ingredients

For the spice rub

- ❖ 1 tsp. cayenne pepper
- ❖ 1 Tbs. Kosher salt
- ❖ 3 garlic cloves, minced
- ❖ 2 Tbs. smoked paprika
- ❖ 2 tsp. dried oregano
- ❖ 1 ½ tsp. ground black pepper
- ❖ 1/4 cup raw turbinado sugar
- ❖ ¼ cup fresh parsley, minced

For the Balsamic BBQ Sauce

- ❖ 1 1/2 cups ketchup
- ❖ ¾ cup balsamic vinegar
- ❖ 1 red onion, minced
- ❖ ¾ cup maple syrup
- ❖ 1 garlic clove, minced
- ❖ ½ cup apple cider vinegar
- ❖ 1 serrano chile, minced

For the Seitan Ribs

- ❖ 3 Tbs. dried garlic powder
- ❖ 2 cups vital wheat gluten
- ❖ ¼ cup tahini
- ❖ ¼ cup nutritional yeast
- ❖ 2 cups water
- ❖ ½ tsp. ground black pepper
- ❖ ¼ cup low-sodium soy sauce

- ❖ 3 Tbs. Mexican chile powder
- ❖ 3 Tbs. dried onion powder
- ❖ 2 tsp. liquid smoke

Directions

1. Add the spice rub ingredients in a small bowl. Stir and let it sit for now.
2. In another bowl mix together, apple cider vinegar, chile, balsamic vinegar, red onion, maple syrup, garlic, and ketchup. Mix well and add to a pan.
3. Cook on low heat for an hour or so and add some water if preferred.
4. Preheat the oven to 375 degrees F.
5. Add the dry ingredients in a mixing bowl and mix. Add in the wet ingredients one by one and mix well. This would create dough.
6. Roll out the dough and cut into 15 thick ribs.
7. Add to the baking dish and use the spice rub to flavor it.
8. Bake for about 1 hour.
9. Brush the ribs using the sauce and bake for another 12 minutes.
10. To make the Tempeh Ribs, cut the tempeh in 8 rectangles.
11. Steam them carefully for 20 minutes or so.
12. Add the spice rub and arrange on a baking tray.
13. Bake until it becomes brown. It may take 20 minutes.
14. Brush the bbq sauce and bake for another 5 minutes.

71. **Seitan "Roast Beef"**

Ingredients

- ❖ 1/2 onion, minced
- ❖ 2 t browning liquid
- ❖ 2 cups mushrooms
- ❖ 1 t liquid smoke
- ❖ 2 c vital wheat gluten
- ❖ 2 t Worcestershire sauce
- ❖ 1 T garlic powder
- ❖ 3 t evoo
- ❖ Small handful dried porcinis with liquid
- ❖ 1/4 c nutritional yeast
- ❖ 1/2 cup tvp soaked in 1/2 hot veg broth

Simmering liquid

- ❖ 1/4 soy sauce
- ❖ 5 c vegetable broth
- ❖ couple dashes Worcestershire and liquid smoke
- ❖ 1/2 c tomato sauce
- ❖ any leftover mushroom liquid
- ❖ 1/2 c vinegar

Directions

1. In a skillet heat the oil and fry the onion with mushroom for 10 minutes.

2. Add the vinegar and cook for 8 minutes.

3. Add the mushroom broth and cook for another 15 minutes.

4. In a bowl combine the garlic, yeast, gluten, and knead well.

5. Mix well and add the liquid smoke, browning liquid and the rest of the ingredients.
6. Mix well and add to the skillet.
7. Toss for 5 minutes and take off the heat. Add to a baking dish.
8. Bake for 45 minutes with 350 degrees F.

72. Sweet Potatoes Burgers With Veggie Fries

Serves 5

Ingredients

Burgers

- ❖ 1 red bell pepper, diced
- ❖ 1 yam, diced
- ❖ 5 tablespoons ground flax seeds
- ❖ Salt and pepper to taste
- ❖ 4 tablespoons nutritional yeast
- ❖ Cumin to taste
- ❖ 4 large mushrooms, sliced
- ❖ 2/3 cup green onions, diced
- ❖ 4 dates, diced
- ❖ Fresh herbs
- ❖ 4 garlic cloves, minced
- ❖ A pinch of turmeric and paprika

Fries

- ❖ 1 jicama root, sliced
- ❖ 1 teaspoon veg oil
- ❖ Salt and pepper to taste
- ❖ Cumin to taste
- ❖ Fresh herbs
- ❖ A pinch of turmeric and paprika

Ketchup

- ❖ Salt (to taste)
- ❖ 1/2 cup sun dried tomatoes
- ❖ 3 dates

- ❖ 1-2 tomatoes
- ❖ Water

Directions

1. Add all the vegetables and herbs, spices in a blender.
2. Blend until it is well mixed.
3. Transfer to a bowl and create flat burger patties.
4. Coat the jicama with oil, salt, turmeric, paprika, herbs and cumin.
5. Fry them golden brown.
6. Add the ketchup ingredients in a blender and blend into a smooth mixture.
7. Fry the burgers golden brown.
8. Serve everything together.

73. Falafel with Coconut Yogurt Nut Sauce

Ingredients

- ❖ 1 18 oz can cooked chick peas
- ❖ 1/5 cup parsley
- ❖ 1/3 cup onion, chopped
- ❖ 1/2 cup bread crumbs
- ❖ 1/4 cup cilantro, chopped
- ❖ 1 1/2 teaspoon cumin
- ❖ 1 small garlic clove
- ❖ 1/2 teaspoon salt
- ❖ tahini sauce
- ❖ 1 tablespoon lemon juice
- ❖ 1/2 cup coconut yogurt
- ❖ 1 tablespoons tahini

Directions

For the Falafel

1. In a blender, add the chickpeas, onions, bread crumbs, cilantro, all the spices and salt. Blend well and create round falafel.
2. Fry them golden brown with oil.
3. Serve with yogurt sauce.

For the Tahini Sauce

4. Combine the yogurt, tahini and lemon juice in a bowl and mix well.

74. Healthy Bean Patties

Ingredients

- ❖ 1/4 cup flour
- ❖ 2 cups white beans
- ❖ 1 celery stalk, chopped fine
- ❖ 1/2 tsp paprika
- ❖ 2 scallions chopped thin
- ❖ 1/2 tsp salt or to taste
- ❖ 1/2 tsp cumin
- ❖ 1 small carrot, chopped fine
- ❖ 1/4 tsp thyme leaf
- ❖ Fresh ground pepper to taste
- ❖ 2 minced garlic cloves
- ❖ 1 Tbsp minced fresh ginger
- ❖ 1 Tbsp olive oil
- ❖ 2 Tbsp chopped parsley
- ❖ 1 cup fine dry breadcrumbs

Directions

1. Fry the vegetables with oil for 10 minutes.
2. Add the rest of the ingredients and toss for 5 minutes.
3. Transfer the mixture to a strong food processor.
4. Blend until the mixture is coarse.
5. Create patties and fry them golden brown.

75. Falafel with a Twist

Ingredients

- ❖ 1 cup cooked chickpeas
- ❖ 1/4 cup breadcrumbs
- ❖ 1/4 cup packed fresh cilantro
- ❖ 3 large garlic cloves
- ❖ 1/4 cup ground flax
- ❖ 3 tbsp fresh lemon juice
- ❖ 1/2 tsp ground cumin
- ❖ 1/2 cup red onion, roughly chopped
- ❖ 1/4 cup packed fresh parsley
- ❖ 1/2 tsp fine grain sea salt

Directions

1. In a blender add the chickpeas, garlic, onion, and blend well.
2. Add the herbs, lemon juice and blend again for 20 seconds.
3. Transfer the mix to a mixing bowl.
4. Add in the rest of the ingredients.
5. Mix well and using your hands, make small falafel.
6. In a skillet heat some oil and add the falafel.
7. Fry them brown and serve with any salad or sauce of your choice.

76. Seitan Roast Vegan Meat and Potatoes

Ingredients

- ❖ 1 cup unbleached white flour
- ❖ 2 teaspoons ginger, roughly chopped
- ❖ 1 small white onion, chopped
- ❖ 4-5 cloves garlic, roughly chopped
- ❖ 2 teaspoons fresh thyme leaves
- ❖ 3 cups vegetable stock
- ❖ 1/4 cup Braggs
- ❖ 2 Tablespoons extra virgin olive oil
- ❖ 3/4 teaspoon salt
- ❖ 1 Tablespoon sesame oil
- ❖ 1 teaspoon dried oregano leaves
- ❖ 4-5 cups vital wheat gluten
- ❖ 1 teaspoon fresh cracked pepper

Directions

1. In a wok fry the onion with olive oil.
2. Add the garlic and fry until brown.
3. Add to a blender with thyme, salt, sesame oil, pepper, tamari and half of the broth.
4. Blend well and add half of the mixture to a bowl.
5. In another bowl add the dry ingredients.
6. Add in the vegetable broth thyme mixture to it and mix well.
7. Create dough and add to a greased loaf pan.
8. Add the rest of the thyme broth mix on top.

9. Bake in the oven for 1 hour with 300^0 F.

77. <u>Homemade Seitan</u>

Ingredients

- ❖ 4 cups cold water
- ❖ 4 cups white flour
- ❖ 3 cups whole wheat flour
- ❖ 6 cups vegetable stock

Directions

1. Combine the flours in a mixing bowl.
2. Add the cold water to it.
3. Knead well and create dough. Create little balls.
4. Bring the vegetable stock to boil in a pot.
5. Add the balls in the vegetable stock and cook with the lid for about 1 hour.

78. <u>Vegan sausages with sriracha and five-spice powder</u>

Ingredients

- ❖ 1/2 cup refried beans
- ❖ 1 head of roasted garlic, pureed
- ❖ 2 cups vital wheat gluten
- ❖ 2 TB sriracha
- ❖ 1 TB hot chili oil
- ❖ 1 tsp fennel seed
- ❖ fresh or dried thai chilis
- ❖ 1 tsp liquid smoke
- ❖ 1 TB vegan Worcestershire sauce
- ❖ 1 small shallot, grated
- ❖ 1 TB soy sauce
- ❖ 1 tsp smoked paprika
- ❖ 3 TB chickpea flour
- ❖ 1/2 tsp Chinese Five-Spice powder
- ❖ 1 1/2 cups cold vegetable broth
- ❖ Toasted sesame oil

Directions

1. In a mixing bowl combine the beans, sriracha, spice powder, thai chilis, chili oil, shallot, liquid smoke and garlic.
2. Pour in the cold broth and mix.
3. Add the sauce and soy sauce and the rest of the ingredients. Mix well.
4. Create four different pieces of the mix and roll them out.

5. Add toasted sesame oil in the middle and add the sausage on the top.

6. Twist the roll and seal carefully.

7. Arrange them onto a steaming basket and steam for about 1 hour.

<u>Important Recommendations!</u>

I put in a few product recommendations that I personally use and are great for making every dish as delicious and as healthy as possible. I have been using many of the products for years and can truly vouch for them.

Click on the Link Below To See the Recommendations:

http://bit.ly/2plantbased